Primary Partners

ACHIEVEMENT DAYS

for Girls Ages 8-11

24 Fun Activities with:
☐ Invitations
☐ Goal Projects
☐ Learning Games
☐ Success Snacks

5 Great Theme Parties!
Pop Into the Future!
Soar to Success!
Dad and Me Western Jamboree
Mom and Miss Pig-nic
Burstin' with Pride!

Printed in the United States of America
 Third Printing October 1999
 Fourth Printing December 2000
 Fifth Printing October 2001
Primary Partners: Achievement Days - Ages 8-11

Covenant Communications, Inc.
American Fork, Utah

ISBN 1-55503-989-8

INTRODUCTION
Fun Ways to Achievement Days

Achievement Days is for girls ages 8-11 to achieve goals in 12 areas:

♥ Arts and Crafts ♥ Education and Scholarship ♥ Family History

♥ Family Skills ♥ Health and Personal Grooming ♥ Hospitality

♥ Outdoor Fun and Skills ♥ Personal Preparedness

♥ Safety and Emergency Preparedness ♥ Service and Citizenship

♥ Spirituality ♥ Sports and Physical Fitness

With this *Primary Partners* volume of *Fun Ways to Achievement Days*, you can jump right into a year's worth of theme-coordinated goal activities. You'll find 24 goals to achieve and five parties and incentive activities to motivate and reward girls for goals achieved.

SEND-OFF PARTIES: Pop Into the Future! and Soar with Success! to introduce Achievement Days goals, create an awards bandelo and poster, create an activity journal/workbook with calendars and divider pages to organize goals, and more.

BI-WEEKLY ACTIVITIES: Twice a month enjoy goal Achievement Days Activities. Allow girls to help with: Invitations, goal activity presentation, games, and Success Snacks. If girls are encouraged to take on leadership responsibilities, they gain confidence and develop their social skills at the same time. Simply copy the activity plans and delegate tasks two weeks in advance. They can report to you the week before. Girls can organize their assignments and goal plans with a monthly calendar.

SUPPLIES: Simple supplies are suggested, and activities are designed to limit expenses. We suggest you purchase one set of markers girls can share. The washable markers are best as they color lightly over illustrations so the images show through. Use Rubbermaid Contact® peel-and-apply paper to laminate at home.

REWARD ACTIVITIES: Treat girls to a Dad-and-Me Western Jamboree!, Mom and Miss Pig-nic, and a Bustin' Buttons! award presentation at the end of the year.

BE FLEXIBLE: The activities are designed to give you ideas, not to limit your own creativity.

TIME TESTED ACTIVITIES: The activities in this book were tested during a two-year period with 9-10-year-old girls, each activity lasting 1 1/2-2 hours. You too can Soar to Success with the girls. Enjoy!

More Fun Ways to Achievement Days
Primary Partners
Quick-and-Easy Ways to
Achievement Days for Girls Ages 8-11
Available in Book and CD-ROM to Print Images in Full-color or Black and White

You'll Find:

24 Goal Activities with Invitations, Icebreaker Activities, Goal Activities, and Success Snacks. They Are:

- *Arts and Crafts:* Drawing Fun!, I'm "Sew" Happy!
- *Education & Scholarship:* Coloring My Life with Knowledge, Super Study Spot
- *Family History:* Scrap Happy Scrapbook Fun!, "Meet My Ancestor" Spotlight
- *Family Skills:* Dough Art from the Heart, Sparkle and Shine!
- *Health & Personal Grooming:* Beauty Shop Hair Talk, Healthy Food Fun!
- *Hospitality:* Mending and Keeping Friendship, It's Party Time!
- *Outdoor Fun & Skills:* Splish, Splash Water Fun and Safety, Outdoor Cookout
- *Personal Preparedness:* Turn Over a New Leaf, Bloom Where You're Planted
- *Safety & Emergency Preparedness:* Ladybug, Ladybug Fly Away Home, Stranger Danger
- *Service & Citizenship:* Scatter Sunshine, Senior Service
- *Spirituality:* Gospel Standards Help Me, Sunday Fun Activities
- *Sports & Physical Fitness:* Heart Smart Workout, Flip Over Old Fashioned Games

Fun Theme Parties!:
- Zap Boredom with Zippy Achievement Days
- Buttons and Bows Daddy Daughter Date
- Dress and Dazzle! Mom and Me Fashion Show

Quarterly Motivation and Award Activities:
- Fishing for Success!
- Clowning Around Carnival
- Hats Off to You!
- You're the Star!

TABLE OF CONTENTS

Party #1 Theme: Pop into the Future!

OBJECTIVE: Welcome girls and introduce them to the My Achievement Days* book. Girls are to achieve two goals in each of the 12 goal areas.

YOU'LL NEED: Give each girl a copy of My Achievement Days book*, and copy the following patterns #1-3 on colored cardstock paper: Pattern #1 Invitation, name tag, and straw decoration (page 2), Pattern #2 Soda pop can label (page 3), and Pattern #4 Achievement Days bandelo (pages 4-5),

OPTION: two extra copies of bandelo balloons to cut up for match game, 1 copy of set of POP-QUIZ wordstrips (page 6) on lightweight paper, and supplies.

SUPPLIES: Balloon and three feet of clear contact paper for each girl, pins for name tags, straws, tape, paper punch, 40" of ribbon (to tie 5 bows on bandelo), crayons, pencils, or watercolor markers, and Success Snacks: Can of soda pop, pepperoni pizza, and two-ounce bag of small candy pieces, i.e. M&M's® or Skittles®, or peanuts or almonds (as prizes).

DO AHEAD: Color and create invitation and deliver a week ahead. Cut out Pop-up Quiz wordstrips (page 6), roll up, stuff in balloons, and blow up balloons.

WELCOME girls to Achievement Days by giving them a "My Achievement Days" book*. Tell them that they are to write their goals achieved in this book for all the years, ages 8-12, that they are in Achievement Days.

POP INTO THE FUTURE! ACTIVITY: Give each girls a Pop into the Future! name tag. Have girls take turns reading a page of the My Achievement Days* book to prepare for the Pop-Quiz (see page 6 for details). Have the Pop-Quiz to see what they have learned.

ACHIEVEMENT DAYS BALLOON MATCH GAME: Cut out two sets of balloons into square shapes (see bandelo--pages 4-5). Girls in a circle take turns turning two cards over at a time to guess the area of achievement and make a match. The girl with the most matched cards wins. Girls can shout, "Let's Pop into the Future!"

AWARDS BANDELO OR POSTER: Follow instructions on page 4 to create bandelo to motivate goal achievement. Encourage girls to wear bandelo during most activities. Option to bandelo is My Soar to Success! Award Poster (page 24).

SUCCESS SNACKS: ♥ Pop Into the Future! Soda Pop. Color and laminate the soda pop can label and straw decoration (using clear contact paper). Tape label to the can (making sure you tape bottom, or label slips off and pop can falls to the floor). Punch holes in the straw decoration to place on straw. Talk about the Achievement Days goals and how we can balance our life as Jesus did (Luke 2:52): Ment<u>al</u> (wisdom), Physic<u>al</u> (stature), Spiritu<u>al</u> (favor with God), and Soci<u>al</u> (favor with man). Tell girls that each of these b<u>al</u>anced life areas have an "al" at the end, which show us that all are necessary for a b<u>al</u>anced life.

♥ 12 Ways to Achievement Days Pepperoni Pizza. Serve pizza topped with 12 pepperoni pieces. Before eating, name the 12 Achievement Days goal areas and say, "My Achievement Days goals give my life pizza-zz!"

♥ Pop-Quiz Prize. Award girls with a two-ounce bag of candy, peanuts, or almonds after playing the Pop Into the Future Pop-Quiz activity. Tell girls the candy or nuts can be placed inside the pop can (after it has been washed out and allowed to dry). Then, each time they achieve a goal in Achievement Days they can enjoy a treat.

*My Achievement Days is published by The Church of Jesus Christ of Latter-day Saints, Salt Lake City, Utah.

PATTERN: Party #1 Invitation, name tag, and Success Snack straw decoration

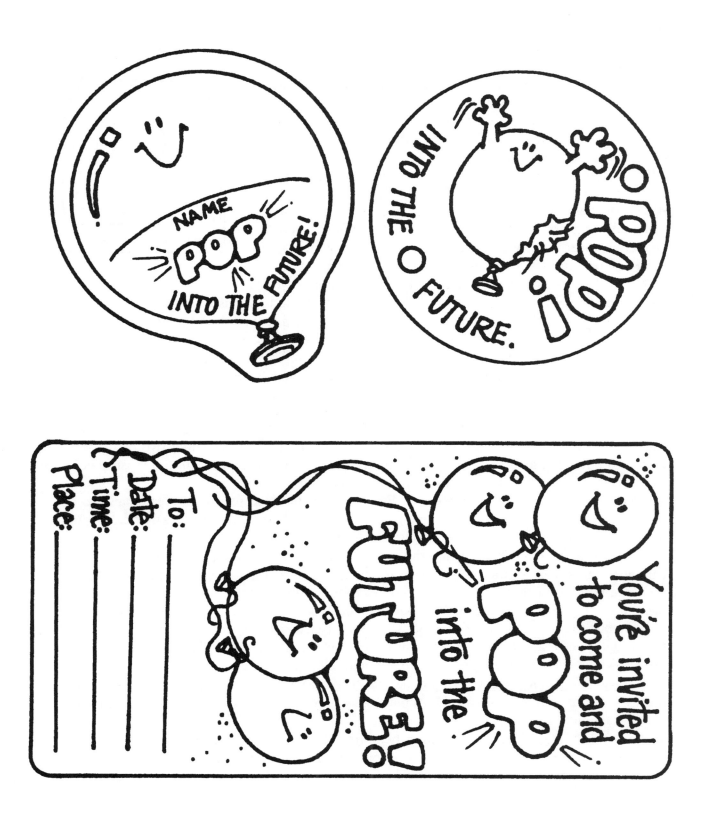

PATTERN: Soda pop can label

TO DECORATE
SODA POP CAN:

1. Copy label on colored cardstock for each girl.

2. Color and cut out invitation and deliver.

3. During the party, have girls color can label and straw decoration without cutting out. Laminate their creations with clear contact paper.

4. If girls brought their photo, glue it to label before laminating, or girls can, tape it on later.

5. See page 6 for details on filling can with candy or nuts to enjoy after each goal is achieved.

6. Cut out can label and tape to soda pop can, making sure you tape to the bottom, as can slips, and pop can spill.

7. Punch holes in straw decoration and place on straw.

I can POP into the future and balance my life like Jesus. LUKE 2:52

Achievement Days bandelo

How to Use Bandelo:
Girls wear bandelo to remind them of their Achievement Days goals. Reward girls for goals achieved by gluing a jewel, sewing a sequin or pearl on the balloon area for each goal achieved.

How to Make Bandelo:
1. Girls color bandelo balloons with colored pencils or Crayola® BRITE watercolor markers. Write girl's name and glue a recent photo below the word "bandelo".
2. Laminate or cover with Rubber Maid Clear Con-Tact® paper.
3. Cut out and punch holes.
4. Tie bandelo together with ribbon, placing the Achievement Days strip in the center back. Place goal balloons for #1-6 in the front and #7-12 in the back.

Recognition Ideas:
1. At the end of the year or beginning of a new year, have the girls wear their bandelos to Primary or at a special party to recognize girls for goals achieved.
2. Each girl could tell about one goal achieved.
3. Award each girl with a certificate (page 152).
4. Have girls decorate balloons to match the 12 balloons to decorate a banquet or treat table.
5. Take a group photo of girls and leader wearing bandelos. See acknowledgement page ii.

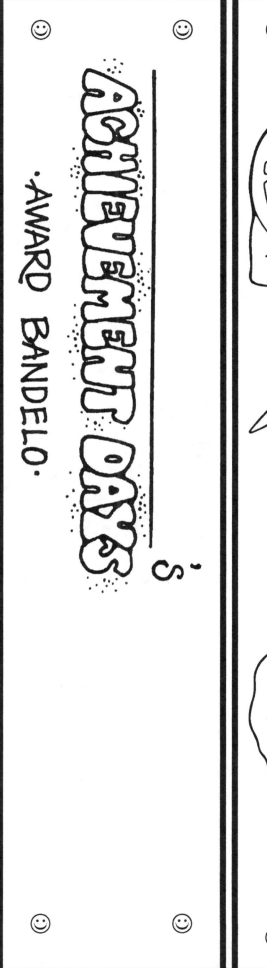

PATTERN: Pop Into the Future! POP-UP QUIZ ♥ **TO MAKE:** Copy 1 set on lightweight paper. Cut out and roll up individual wordstrips to place inside balloons, i.e. place two or three in each balloon. Blow up balloon and tie.

OBJECTIVE: To preview My Achievement Days book* and
to test the girls' knowledge of the Achievement Day goals.

TO START: Have all girls bounce balloons in the air as they say: "I Can Soar to Success with Achievement Days!" Then sit down with My Achievement Days book* in hand and read the ideas for the 12 goal areas.

POP-UP QUIZ:
1. Divide girls into two teams sitting across from their opposing team.
2. Girls take turns sitting on a balloon and reading the wordstrips aloud, saying the number first. Girls can spontaneously guess the goal achievement area, i.e. Arts and Crafts. Leader looks at the number (see answers below) to see if they are correct. Girls look at the list of subjects found in the My Achievement Days* book. The first girl to guess correctly wins a point for her team (leader keeps score).

PRIZES:
1. Stop after playing with half of the balloons. Give winning team a 2-ounce bag of small candy pieces or nuts to place inside the pop can used for the Success Snack (see page @).
2. Tell girls they can eat a treat after each goal is achieved throughout the year. Encourage them to rinse out the can and let it dry before adding the candy pieces or nuts.
3. Give treats to the losing team of girls and play until all balloons are popped and wordstrips read.

WORDSTRIPS TO PLACE INSIDE BALLOONS:

1. Make a handicraft item.	2. Create, collect, and display objects.	3. Write and perform a play or story.
4. Improve personal study habits.	5. Improve grades in one subject.	6. Plan to go to library to read.
7. Learn of educational places.	8. Share life history of a relative.	9. Keep a journal and personal records.
10. Prepare a family group sheet.	11. Keep a 4-generation pedigree chart.	12. Learn child-care skills.
13. Learn to repair things at home.	14. Cook and serve good meals.	15. Do a family home evening lesson.
16. Avoid strong drink and drugs.	17. Learn good health habits.	18. Learn to be clean and groomed.
19. Dress modestly and neatly.	20. Learn how to be a good friend.	21. Learn manners and courtesy.
22. Practice hospitality skills/manners.	23. Learn to introduce special guests.	24. Build and cook on a fire.
25. Go on a nature hike.	26. Learn and use a compass.	27. Preserve your environment.
28. Plan and schedule your time.	29. Make a budget and savings plan.	30. Plant, weed, and harvest a garden.
31 (or 4). Learn about career skills.	32. Learn first-aid skills.	33. Learn disaster survival skills.
34. Learn personal safety rules.	35. Know what to do if lost.	36. Learn and obey laws of the land.
37. Participate in a flag ceremony.	38. Help and visit elderly or sick.	39. Make a nursery toy to donate.
40. Share the gospel with others.	41. Memorize Articles of Faith.	42. Tell scripture stories.
43. Visit a temple visitors' center.	44. Play sports activities in your area.	45. Practice sportsmanship at an event.
46. Learn how to be physically fit.	47. Plan a personal exercise program	FREE POINT

ANSWERS to POP-UP QUIZ:

#1-3 Arts & Crafts	#4-7 Education and Scholarship	#8-11 Family History
#12-15 Family Skills	#16-19 Health and Grooming	#20-23 Hospitality
#24-27 Outdoor Fun and Skills	#28-31 Personal Preparedness	#32-35 Safety & Emer. Preparedness
#36-39 Service and Citizenship	#40-43 Spirituality	#44-47 Sports and Physical Fitness

Party #2 Theme: Soar to Success with Achievement Days

OBJECTIVE: Help girls set up a journal or notebook to store Achievement Days activities, plan and organize goal activities.

YOU'LL NEED: Copies of the following for each girl on cardstock paper:
1. Invitation (page 8)
2. My Achievement Days journal page (page 9)
3. 12 Achievement Days journal dividers (pages 10-21)
4. Divider tabs (page 22)
5. 2 sets of goal reward glue-on stickers (page 23--on colored lightweight paper)
6. My Soar to Success! poster (page 24) or use bandelo (pages 4-5)
7. A-Z Me (page 25)
8. Calendar posters (pages 26-37)
9. 12 of the basic My Achievement Days Calendar (page 38)
10. 1 set of balloon glue-on stickers (page 39) to place on My Achievement Days Calendar

SUPPLIES: Scissors, 3-ringed binder, three 8 1/2" x 11" plastic sheet protectors and one 8 1/2" x 11" sheet of clear contact paper (purchase at grocery store) for each girl, crayons, pencils, or markers, and Success Snacks below or suggestion on page 151).

INVITATION: Color, cut out, and deliver invitation. Give each girl 12 calendar pages to enter dates and months to bring to the activity.

ACHIEVEMENT DAYS JOURNAL: Create a journal using a 3-ring binder (girls are asked to bring binder on the invitation).
1. Color and enclose My Achievement Days journal (page 9) inside a plastic sheet protector (or laminate and glue on front of binder).
2. Color and punch 12 Achievement Days journal divider pages (pages 10-21) and place in binder.
3. Laminate divider tabs with clear contact paper, cut out tabs, and help girls tape tabs to pages.
4. Each Achievement Days, enter Goal #1 or Goal #2 on divider pages. When goals are achieved, reward girls with a glue-on sticker, i.e. "Wow," or "Good Show!" Have parents, Achievement Days leader or Primary president sign and date when goal is complete. Goals completed can be entered in the My Achievement Days booklet*.

MY SOAR TO SUCCESS! AWARDS POSTER: This activity is an alternative to making the bandelo. Have girls color poster and reward them when goals are achieved by gluing or sewing a sequin, jewel, or sticker for each goal achieved. Place this page inside a plastic sheet protector.

A-Z ME!: Girls can place their picture here and enter their favorite people, places, and things. Place this page inside a plastic sheet protector.

ACHIEVEMENT DAYS PLANNING CALENDAR: Create a picture calendar using 12 fun goal posters to motivate goal achievement, and 12 calendars to schedule goals. Option #1--Place calendar in journal or Option #2--spiral bind to hang on wall.
1. Date ahead of time 12 calendar pages (page 38). When you decide which goals you will achieve each month, you can enter goals on the calendar pages.
2. Cut out glue-on balloon stickers (page 39) and glue in the Goal #1 and Goal #2 squares. Balloons should match the two goal activities planned for the month.
3. Place calendar posters (pages 26-37) in front of calendar page for the month.
4. Scheduling Ideas: Outdoor Fun Goal #1 in May to create a window box garden for Mother's Day gift, and Personal Preparedness Goal #1 after this activity.

SUCCESS SNACK: Soar to Success Balloon Cake. Bake a cake in a 9" x 13" cake pan, frost in pan, and place 12 large gumdrops on frosting as balloons. Place frosting in a tube or plastic bag (cutting corner) to decorate frosting balloon strings coming down from large gumdrops, and writing "Soar to Success."

*My Achievement Days is published by The Church of Jesus Christ of Latter-day Saints, Salt Lake City, Utah.

You're invited to come and

SOAR
to
SUCCESS!

To: _____
(Bring a 3-ring binder for a fun, fun activity!)

Date:
_____

Time:
_____

Place:
_____

See you there!

You're invited to come and

SOAR
to
SUCCESS!

To: _____
(Bring a 3-ring binder for a fun, fun activity!)

Date:
_____

Time:
_____

Place:
_____

See you there!

My ACHIEVEMENT DAYS JOURNAL

This belongs to:

_____

ARTS AND CRAFTS

Goal #1:_____

_____

Date Achieved:_____ Signature:_____

Goal #2:_____

_____

Date Achieved:_____ Signature:_____

FAMILY SKILLS

Goal #1: _____

_____

Date Achieved: _____ Signature: _____

Goal #2: _____

_____

Date Achieved: _____ Signature: _____

HEALTH AND PERSONAL GROOMING

Goal #1: _____

_____

Date Achieved: _____ Signature: _____

Goal #2: _____

_____

Date Achieved: _____ Signature: _____

EDUCATION AND SCHOLARSHIP

Goal #1: _____

_____

Date Achieved: _____ Signature: _____

Goal #2: _____

_____

Date Achieved: _____ Signature: _____

FAMILY HISTORY

Goal #1:_____

_____

Date Achieved:_____ Signature:_____

Goal #2:_____

_____

Date Achieved:_____ Signature:_____

HOSPITALITY

Goal #1:_____

_____

Date Achieved:_____ Signature:_____

Goal #2:_____

_____

Date Achieved:_____ Signature:_____

OUTDOOR FUN AND SKILLS

Goal #1: _____
_____

Date Achieved: _____ Signature: _____

Goal #2: _____
_____

Date Achieved: _____ Signature: _____

PERSONAL PREPAREDNESS

Goal #1:_____

_____

Date Achieved:_____ Signature:_____

Goal #2:_____

_____

Date Achieved:_____ Signature:_____

SAFETY AND EMERGENCY PREPAREDNESS

Goal #1: _____

_____

Date Achieved: _____ Signature: _____

Goal #2: _____

_____

Date Achieved: _____ Signature: _____

SERVICE AND CITIZENSHIP

Goal #1:_____

_____

Date Achieved:_____ Signature:_____

Goal #2:_____

_____

Date Achieved:_____ Signature:_____

SPORTS AND PHYSICAL FITNESS

Goal #1: _____

_____

Date Achieved: _____ Signature: _____

Goal #2: _____

_____

Date Achieved: _____ Signature: _____

SPORTS AND PHYSICAL FITNESS

Goal #1:_____

_____

Date Achieved:_____ Signature:_____

Goal #2:_____

_____

Date Achieved:_____ Signature:_____

Divider Tabs for
Achievement Days Divider Pages

HOW TO PLACE TABS ON DIVIDER SHEETS:
1. Copy on colored cardstsock to match divider pages.
2. Cover with clear contact paper to reinforce tabs.
3. Cut out and fold above word line, i.e. fold above "Arts & Crafts."
4. Glue or tape tab on divider page in order (five tabs will show at the same time).

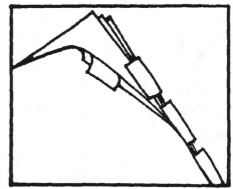

Arts & Crafts	**Education & Scholarship**	**Family History**
Family Skills	**Health & Pers. Grooming**	**Hospitality**
Outdoor Fun & Skills	**Personal Preparedness**	**Safety & Emergency Prep.**
Service & Citizenship	**Spirituality**	**Sports & Physical Fitness**

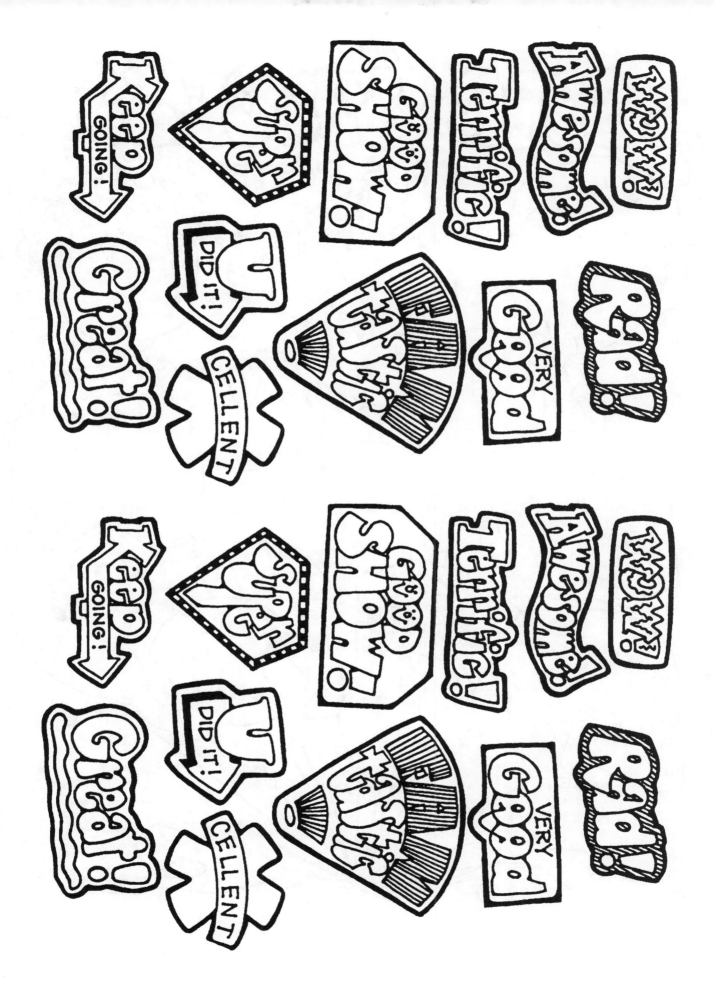

Name: _____ Age: ____ Year: _____

A-Z Me!

My Favorite People, Places, and Things Are:

Actor _____   Hobby _____   Vacation _____

Actress _____   Magazine _____   Vegetable _____

Animal _____   Movie _____   **A-Z Friends--Phone:**

Artist _____   Music _____   _____

Book _____   Quiet Place _____   _____

Candy _____   Sandwich _____   _____

Career _____   Scripture _____   _____

Color _____   Season _____   _____

Cookie _____   Singer _____   _____

Dessert _____   Song _____   _____

Flavor _____   Sport _____   _____

Flower _____   Teacher _____   _____

Food _____   TV Show _____   _____

Fragrance _____

Fruit _____

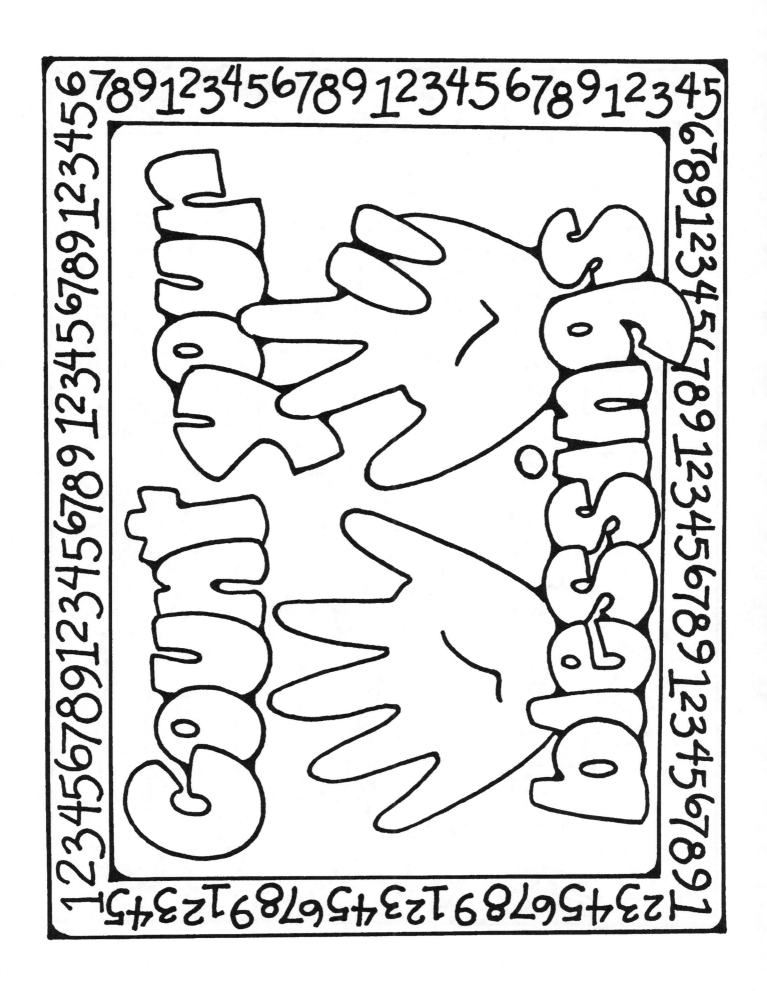

HAPPINESS is a gift that you give to yourself!

Soar to Success! Achievement Days Calendar

MONTH _____ YEAR _____

SUNDAY	MONDAY	TUESDAY	WEDNESDAY	THURSDAY	FRIDAY	SATURDAY

Goal Plans:

Goal Plans:

PATTERN: My Achievement Calendar glue-on stickers ♥ Copy double set for each girl on lightweight paper to glue on monthly planning calendar. Stickers indicate goals planned for the month.

39

Arts & Crafts: Goal #1

Let's Make Pop-ups!
Create two pop-ups and other greeting cards

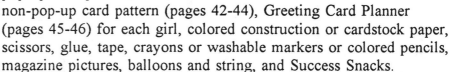

YOU'LL NEED: Copies of pop-up invitation (page 41) on colored cardstock paper, Pop-up Cards and Creations handout, and I Love You pop-up card pattern, and Thank Ewe non-pop-up card pattern (pages 42-44), Greeting Card Planner (pages 45-46) for each girl, colored construction or cardstock paper, scissors, glue, tape, crayons or washable markers or colored pencils, magazine pictures, balloons and string, and Success Snacks.

INVITATIONS: Make and deliver a week ahead.

CREATE POP-UP CARDS: Make ahead samples pop-up designs #1-4 (page 42). Help girls create two pop-up greeting cards. Give girls the I Love You card pattern shown right (page 43).

NON-POP-UP CARDS: Encourage girls to make other cards that are not pop-ups. Give girls the thank you card pattern shown right (page 44).

POETRY: Show girls how to rhyme and create a play on words, i.e.: Buzz on over to our beehive for a look at our "bee"-autiful garden.

GREETING CARD PLANNER: Girls can color and cut out Greeting Card Planner (pages 45-46) and glue pages to a file folder. Then write names and dates by each month and enclose homemade greeting cards made ahead.

POP-UP BALLOON ACTIVITY AND GAME:

ACTIVITY--Poppin' as it Pops: Tape a blown-up balloon on the back of each girl's chair and write one type of greeting card on each balloon with a permanent marker, i.e.: Thank You, Get Well, Happy Birthday, Merry Christmas, Happy Easter, St. Patrick's Day, Halloween, Mother's Day, Father's Day, Anniversary, Graduation, Baby Shower, and Wedding. Balloon can remain on chair while girls create cards. Ask girls to pop the balloons in the air as you pop popcorn. Ask girls to say the names of the greeting cards as they pop balloons in the air. Say: *"Thank You," Get Well,"* and others.

GAME--Balloon Stomp-and-Pop: Girls take off shoes and tie a balloon to their ankle with a string. At the word "GO" girls stop on each other's balloons to have a poppin' good time. Last girl with an unpopped balloon wins!

SUCCESS SNACKS: Soda Pop and Popcorn Treats. ♥ Buttered, ♥ Cheese Flavored (sprinkle with Parmesan cheese), ♥ Caramel Corn: 1 pound (2 1/2 cups) packed brown sugar, 1 cup white corn syrup, 1 cube butter, pinch of salt. Bring to full boil. Add 1 can sweetened condensed milk. Cook to soft ball stage (about 5 minutes). Add 1 teaspoon vanilla, pour 1 gallon popcorn, spread on tray to set.

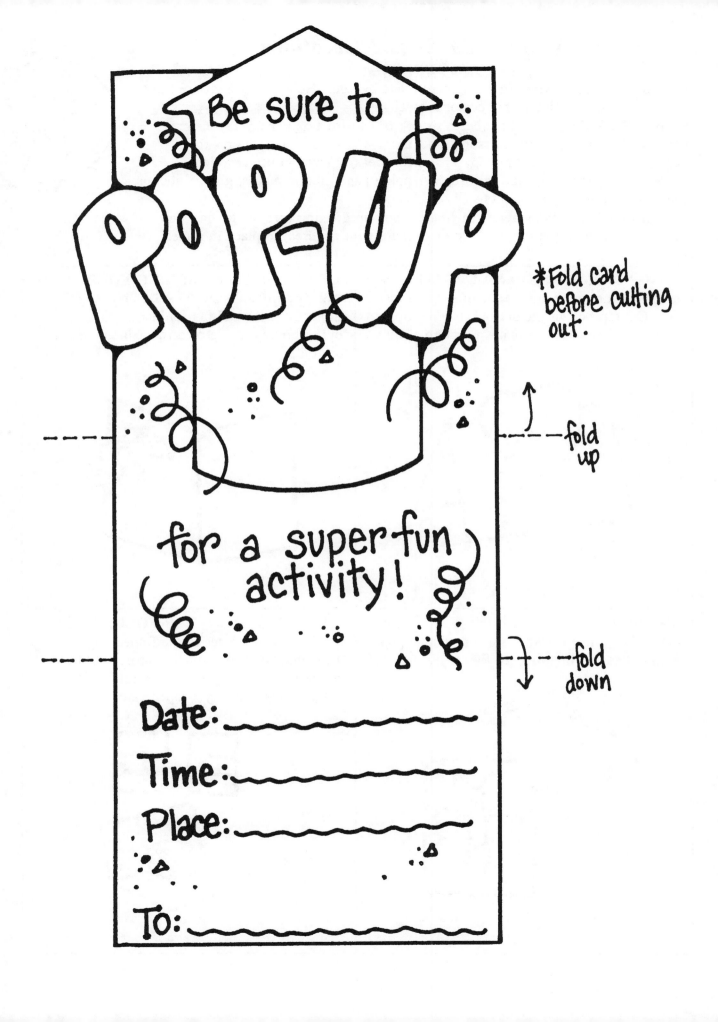

Pop-up Cards and Creations

Let's Make Pop-ups!

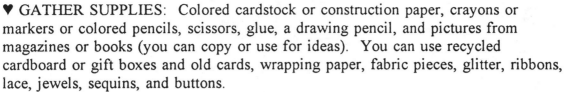

♥ Surprise someone with a greeting card made by you. Homemade cards are fun to make and receive and add that personal touch.

♥ GATHER SUPPLIES: Colored cardstock or construction paper, crayons or markers or colored pencils, scissors, glue, a drawing pencil, and pictures from magazines or books (you can copy or use for ideas). You can use recycled cardboard or gift boxes and old cards, wrapping paper, fabric pieces, glitter, ribbons, lace, jewels, sequins, and buttons.

♥ Follow the instructions below to create a pop-up greeting card, or go one step further and create a pop-up book you can share with children, to place in Super Sitter Kit.

POP-UP DESIGN #1 **STAND-UP:** Fold a card in half. Glue on or draw a picture on the inside left. Cut top half of picture out, leaving bottom half. Fold card back to make a picture stand.	POP-UP DESIGN #2 **SPRING FOLD:** Fold card in half. Cut 2" x 1/2" piece of cardstock paper and fan-fold strip. Glue one fold to bottom inside of card. Glue picture to top fold.

POP-UP DESIGN #3 **CUT IN:** Fold card in half. Cut in image 3/4th through. Image pops out, i.e. bee or bird wing, or flower petal.	POP-UP DESIGN #4 **TAB-FOLD:** Fold card in half. Cut in center of the folded edge 1 1/2" in the middle (two slits--1/2" apart). Cut out picture image. Glue to tab and fold card. Image springs up as you open card.

Pattern:
I Love You
pop-up card

**TO MAKE
CARD:**
1. Color and
cut out pop-
up card.
2. Fold down
center of
heart and cut
on dotted
line.
3. Fold
bottom lines
of heart so
heart leans
out.
4. Fold
between A
and B.
5. Spread
glue on back
side of B and
glue to A.

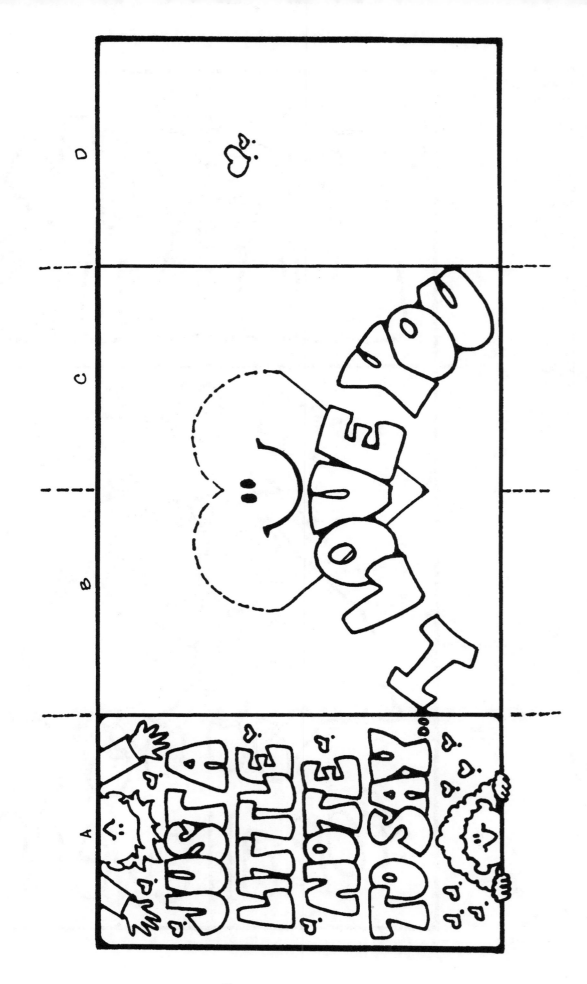

43

Pattern:
Thank you card

TO MAKE CARD:
Color and cut out card. Fan fold and glue front flap to middle. Sign and deliver. Card can be sent to mom or dad, bishop, chorister, special teacher, or friend.

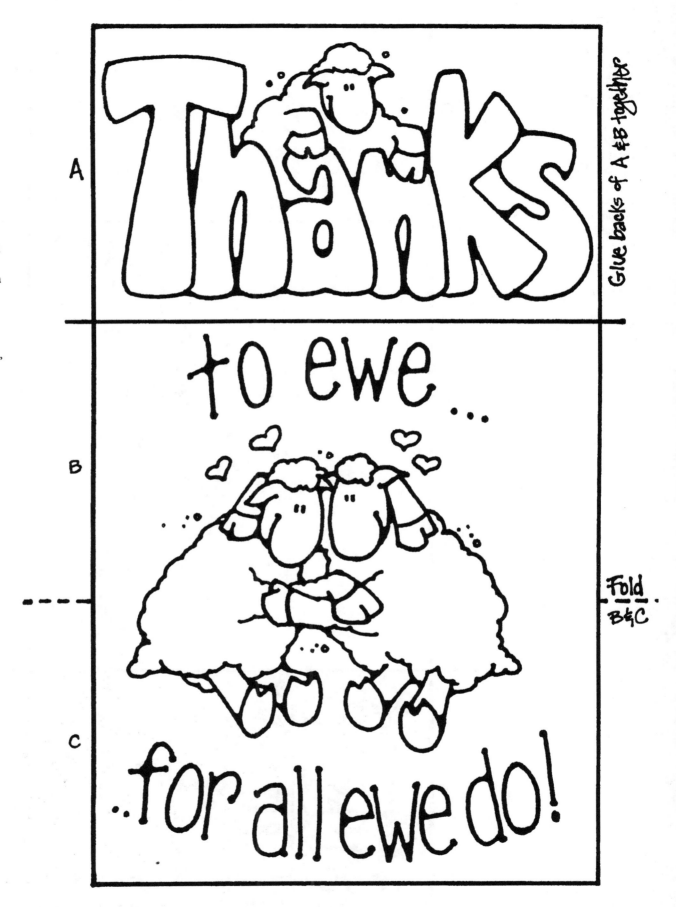

A

Glue backs of A &B together

to ewe ...

B

Fold B&C

C

..for all ewe do!

GLUE PART B HERE.
MAKE SURE TO GLUE
ONLY THE SIDES AND
BOTTOM, LEAVING THE
TOP OPEN TO STORE
CARDS

PART A

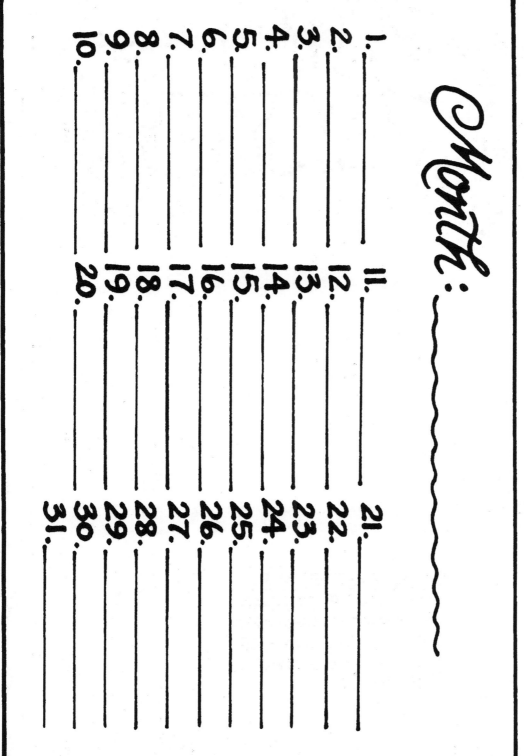

PART B

Month: _____

1. _____   11. _____   21. _____
2. _____   12. _____   22. _____
3. _____   13. _____   23. _____
4. _____   14. _____   24. _____
5. _____   15. _____   25. _____
6. _____   16. _____   26. _____
7. _____   17. _____   27. _____
8. _____   18. _____   28. _____
9. _____   19. _____   29. _____
10. _____   20. _____   30. _____
                                     31. _____

MAKE 12 COPIES
OF PART A & B
FOR EACH GIRL.
(ONE FOR
EVERY MONTH)

Arts & Crafts: Goal #2

You're on Stage! - *Create and Perform a Play*

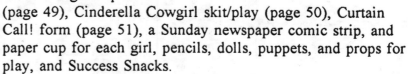

YOU'LL NEED:
Copies of invitation (page 48) on colored cardstock paper, You're in the Limelight cup label (page 49), Cinderella Cowgirl skit/play (page 50), Curtain Call! form (page 51), a Sunday newspaper comic strip, and paper cup for each girl, pencils, dolls, puppets, and props for play, and Success Snacks.

INVITATIONS: Make and deliver a week ahead.

CREATE A DOLL OR PUPPET PLAY:
1. Divide girls into groups of two or three.
2. Ask girls to write their own 5-minute play using dolls, puppets, or finger puppets.
3. Ask girls to write their play on Curtain Call: You're in the Limelight! form (page 51).
4. Give girls 30 minutes to prepare.

CURTAIN CALL:
1. Provide a blanket for the curtain and a mock stage for play.
2. Say to the girls, "Curtain Call! The rehearsal is over ... it's time for the play!"
3. Enjoy watching the plays.

CINDERELLA COWGIRL:
1. Give each girl a copy of the Cinderella Cowgirl play (page 50).
2. Encourage and direct girls to put on this play.
3. Girls can draw names of characters out of a hat.
4. This play could be performed during the Dad and Me Western Jamboree (see page 139).

SUCCESS SNACKS:

IDEA #1 You're In the Limelight Sherbet. Serve lime sherbet in a paper cup with label (page 49). Talk about what they liked about each play presented.

IDEA #2 Limelight Drink: Serve clear soda pop in a paper cup with label (page 49) the following. Pour clear soda pop over green ice cubes. To Make Ice Cubes: Freeze lime punch or color water with green food coloring.

Curtain Call!

It's your chance to be in the limelight and perform on stage!

To:

Date: _____ Time: _____

Place: _____

Bring: Dolls, puppets, and any fun prop.

Curtain Call!

It's your chance to be in the limelight and perform on stage!

To:

Date: _____ Time: _____

Place: _____

Bring: Dolls, puppets, and any fun prop.

PATTERN: paper cup holder to serve <u>You're In the Limelight Sherbet</u> or <u>Limelight Drink</u>

CINDERELLA COWGIRL

Use brooms (stick horses), stuffed toys (animals), orange water balloon (pumpkin), stuffed stocking (mice), ruler (wand), wagon with box (coach), boots (large to slip off easily)

NARRATOR: Cinderella was a rootin' ridin' cowgirl. By rootin' we mean she loved to drink Rootbeer as she rode her favorite horse Tex, named after the state in which she lived. Cinderella was alone most of the time because her stepsister and stepmother didn't want her around. Her father died when she was young. The story begins.

STEP MA: Cinderella! Cinderella! Where's my mornin' grub? Can't you hear me, cowgirl? Get over here and rustle up some vittles! We's hungry! (Cinderella rushes over to help.)

STEPSISTERS: She ain't fast enough, Ma. Let's horsewhip her into shape and make her sleep in the barn next to the coal dust! Then let's go out on the range to feel the cool breeze. It's hot in this here cabin. (Sisters and mother leave, and the cowboy Prince Charming comes riding by.)

PRINCE CHARMING: Hello (looking at Cinderella). Do you have a cool drink of water for a thirsty cowboy?

CINDERELLA: (looks surprised and dreamy-eyed at prince) Sure. We have the best water in Texas! But I'm not sure that I should be seen with you. My stepsisters and ma don't like me giving away this good water.

PRINCE CHARMING: (smiling at Cinderella) Thank you for your kindness. (rides away)

STEP MA: (riding in talking only to the sisters) It's a fine night for a Texas barn dance. It was smart of the Rodeo King and Queen to invite us. The invitation says here that they are lookin' fer a gal fer their cowboy prince charmin' to marry. Well, you gals had better perk up yer ears and put your best dancin' duds on. Let's get ready for the hoe-down! I'm sure one of you will be the next cowgirl princess of Texas.

STEPSISTERS: (looking at Cinderella, who is anxious to go too) You ain't goin', you're just a dirty old cowgirl. You ain't outfitted to go anyhow with those old jeans, and shucks, you got coal dust on your shirt and holes in your boots!

(all exit except Cinderella)

CINDERELLA: (looking sad, until her animal friends pop in) What are you doin' here? Did you come to cheer me up? (The animals bring her fabric and beads.) Oh, is this for me? Maybe I can create a dress to wear. (She puts it together and then starts to cry.) This won't do. I guess I'm here to stay. (She goes to say goodbye to sisters and ma.)

STEPSISTERS: Too bad you don't have anything to wear. You would have such a good time if only you had ... well, if only you looked, ... if only you ...

STEP MA: Girls, hush up. Let's go! (They leave her alone.)

CINDERELLA: (sobs deeply) I wanted to go to the Texas barn dance, and now look at me.

FAIRY GOOD MOTHER: (suddenly pops into the room) It looks like yer a needin' my help, deary. I'm yer Fairy Good Mother, comin' to the rescue. Now perk up girl, go get me a pumpkin and some mice. (With pumpkin and mice in hand, she waves her wand.) Zippity-zappity-zoo!

CINDERELLA: (puts on a nice shirt and vest and boots) The pumpkin is a coach! The mice are horses! And look at me! I look right nice! Thank you, Fairy Good Mother! (gets into coach and rides off)

ANNOUNCER: (plays guitar singing) Here's a new face that the prince hasn't seen. Let's get on with the dancin' and see if she is keen!

CINDERELLA: (walks in and looks at the prince) Howdy!

PRINCE: Would you like to dance? (holds out his arm) Haven't I seen you somewhere before? (They dance and dance and smile.)

CINDERELLA: (clock bongs midnight and she runs away saying) I have to go! Thanks!

PRINCE: (running after her, picking up the cowgirl boot that fell off her) I want to see you again! Wait!

CINDERELLA: (at home in rags, takes off nice vest and shirt; with old shirt underneath, and sits by the fire with one boot on, looking at boot) I knew it was too good to last.

PRINCE: (knocks at door with boot in hand and Cinderella answers) Would you wear this boot and be my bride? Yes!!! Forever! (hug)

Curtain Call: You're in the Limelight!

Goal: Write and perform a five-minute play using form below. Use 15 minutes to write and 15 minutes to practice. Then Curtain Call! The rehearsal is over ... it's time for the play! Curtain can go down after each scene to change props. Use dolls and puppets as characters.

William Shakespeare, Playwright, said:
"All the world is a stage, And all the men and women merely players; They have their exits and their entrances, And one man in his time plays many parts ... "
- *As You Like It ACT II, SCENE 7, LINE 140*

TITLE OF PLAY:	
Narrator's Introduction: Setting:	
CHARACTERS:	DIALOGUE (what characters say and do):

Education & Scholarship: Goal #1

Wishin' in the Wishin' Well: *Choose two careers*

You're invited to come a wishin, in the wishin' well! Date: Time: Place:

Bring the bag of pennies to the activity. See you there!

Wishin' in the Wishin' Well!

YOU'LL NEED: Copies of invitation (page 58) on colored cardstock paper, Wishin' Well Career Checklist (page 53), 10 pennies, and a zip-close plastic bag for each girl, double-stick tape, crayons or washable markers, and Success Snacks.

INVITATIONS: Make and deliver a week ahead. Place 10 pennies in a zip-close plastic bag and double-stick tape it to the invitation. Girls are asked to bring bag to the activity to wish in the wishing well.

CAREER TALK: Have someone talk to girls about their career, schooling for specific careers, and good study habits that make learning fun.

WISHIN' WELL CAREER CHECK:

1. Give each girl a Wishin' Well Career Checklist (page 53), and ask them to check careers that interest them.

2. Help girls memorize: *"Some drink freely from the fountain of knowledge, while others only gargle."*

3. Have girls draw themselves in their Career Choices #1 and #2. The asterisk (*) is placed by careers that could be home-based.

4. Create a wishing well (large shallow bowl of water) into which girls can toss a penny over their shoulder from approximately 5 feet away.

5. Girls can try 10 times, saying, "I wish to be a (career choice)," tossing penny over their shoulder. If girls miss the wishing well after 10 tries, allow them another try, after all girls have tried.

HOMEMAKING: Tell girls that being a homemaker, taking care of the home, meals, and children is a career every girl can enjoy now and when they are married.

SUCCESS SNACK: Wishin' Well Wafer Cookies. For each well you will need six 1 3/4" x 1 1/4" wafer cookies. Purchase wafer cookies with frosting inside two wafers. With extra frosting--glue four wafer cookies together for well base. Press toothpicks into two for well room, pressing toothpicks into well base (illustration right). Before girls eat wishin' well, ask them to make one success wish to the girl on their right. Then say, "A wish is only a wish until I make it come true."

Wishin' Well Career Checklist:
"Some drink freely from the fountain of knowledge, while others only gargle."

A-Z Possible Me:
- ☐ Accountant*
- ☐ Actress ☐ Architect*
- ☐ Baker or Caterer*
- ☐ Banker
- ☐ Bookkeeper*
- ☐ Chef* ☐ Chiropractor
- ☐ Chemist ☐ Clothing Designer ☐ Computer Programmer*
- ☐ Cosmetologist*
- ☐ Crafter*
- ☐ Day Care* ☐ Dancer
- ☐ Doctor ☐ Dance Instructor* ☐ Dentist
- ☐ Detective ☐ Dietitian
- ☐ Display Artist
- ☐ Engineer
- ☐ Fitness Trainer*
- ☐ Flight Attendant
- ☐ Freelance Writer*
- ☐ Graphic Artist*

☐ Illustrator ☐ Interior Decorator* ☐ Lawyer ☐ Librarian ☐ Loan Officer ☐ Maid Service ☐ Manicurist* ☐ Musician ☐ Music Teacher ☐ Nurse ☐ Party or Reunion Planner* ☐ Pet Sitter/Groomer* ☐ Paralegal ☐ Pilot ☐ Pre-school Teacher ☐ Pharmacist ☐ Piano Teacher* ☐ Photographer* ☐ Physical Therapist ☐ Psychiatrist ☐ Psychologist ☐ Radio or TV announcer ☐ Real Estate Agent ☐ Receptionist ☐ Recreation ☐ Reporter ☐ Retail Buyer ☐ Retail Sales Clerk ☐ Seamstress* ☐ Secretary ☐ Scientist ☐ Social Worker ☐ Teacher ☐ Translator ☐ Travel Agent ☐ Typist* ☐ Veterinarian

Drawings of Myself at My Careers #1 and #2: .... *Star (*) the home career.*

Career #1 _____	Career #2 _____

10 PENNIES FOR MY THOUGHTS:
Which careers did I choose to earn that extra cash?
I can make a wish in the wishin' well, by tossing a penny over my shoulder (into a bowl of water), saying, "I will be a _____ _____ (career choice)." I will remember that education is the key to a bright future, and a wish is only a wish until I make it come true.

Wishin' Well Career Checklist:

"Some drink freely from the fountain of knowledge, while others only gargle."

A-Z Possible Me:
- ☐ Accountant*
- ☐ Actress ☐ Architect*
- ☐ Baker or Caterer*
- ☐ Banker
- ☐ Bookkeeper*
- ☐ Chef* ☐ Chiropractor
- ☐ Chemist ☐ Clothing Designer ☐ Computer Programmer*
- ☐ Cosmetologist*

- ☐ Crafter*
- ☐ Day Care* ☐ Dancer
- ☐ Doctor ☐ Dance Instructor* ☐ Dentist
- ☐ Detective ☐ Dietitian
- ☐ Display Artist
- ☐ Engineer
- ☐ Fitness Trainer*
- ☐ Flight Attendant
- ☐ Freelance Writer*
- ☐ Graphic Artist*

☐ Illustrator ☐ Interior Decorator* ☐ Lawyer ☐ Librarian ☐ Loan Officer
☐ Maid Service ☐ Manicurist* ☐ Musician ☐ Music Teacher ☐ Nurse
☐ Party or Reunion Planner* ☐ Pet Sitter/Groomer* ☐ Paralegal ☐ Pilot
☐ Pre-school Teacher ☐ Pharmacist ☐ Piano Teacher* ☐ Photographer*
☐ Physical Therapist ☐ Psychiatrist ☐ Psychologist ☐ Radio or TV announcer
☐ Real Estate Agent ☐ Receptionist ☐ Recreation ☐ Reporter ☐ Retail Buyer
☐ Retail Sales Clerk ☐ Seamstress* ☐ Secretary ☐ Scientist ☐ Social Worker
☐ Teacher ☐ Translator ☐ Travel Agent ☐ Typist* ☐ Veterinarian

Drawings of Myself at My Careers #1 and #2: . . . . *Star (*) the home career.*

Career #1 _____

Career #2 _____

10 PENNIES FOR MY THOUGHTS:
Which careers did I choose to earn that extra cash?
I can make a wish in the wishin' well, by tossing a penny over my shoulder (into a bowl of water), saying, "I will be a _____ (career choice)." I will remember that education is the key to a bright future, and a wish is only a wish until I make it come true.

Education & Scholarship: Goal #2

Be a Jelly Bean Reader:
Learn about fiction and non-fiction books

YOU'LL NEED: Copies of invitation (page 58) and jelly bean match cards (pages 55-56) on colored cardstock paper, and I Have Bean Reading! calendar glue-on stickers (page 57), a zip-close plastic bag and 21 jelly beans for each girl, washable markers, and Success Snacks.

INVITATIONS: Make and deliver a week ahead.

JOIN THE STUDY SCENE WITH JELLY BEANS!

Activity #1 **Library Scene:** Call your local library to arrange a half-hour tour. Ask librarian to point out the difference between fiction and non-fiction books and where to find them. Fiction Books: Short stories, novels (i.e. mysteries, romance, westerns, science fiction, historical), and children's stories. Non-Fiction Books: Nature, history, autobiographies and biographies, humor, cookbooks, music books, reference books (i.e. dictionary, thesaurus, and encyclopedias), art, poetry, how-to books (i.e. repairs and building, science, activity books and parties, home decoration) ... and more. Encourage each girl to get her own library card.

Activity #2 **Reading to Children:** Have girls select a book they would like to read to children. Have several children available for story time.

Activity #3 **Career Jelly Bean Match Game:** Color and cut out one or two sets of match cards to play game. To play: Turn matching cards face down and take turns turning cards over to make a match. As a girl makes a match, have her guess whether the bean book subject is fiction or non-fiction.

Activity #4 **I Have Bean Reading! Rewards:** Challenge girls to read 15 minutes daily for 21 days. It takes 21 days to develop a habit, and the habit of reading has a lifetime of rewards. It allows your mind to expand and become open for even more ideas. The more you learn, the more you want to learn. The habit of reading has great rewards: 1) The more you read, the better reader you become and the easier it is to read, and 2) You have more to talk about, so you become more confident and an interesting person to be around. Give each girl a zip-close plastic bag with 21 jelly beans and a copy of the I Have Bean Reading! glue-on stickers. Tell girls they can eat a jelly bean each day they read 15 minutes and glue a sticker on their calendar on the days they read.

Activity #5 **Education is a Cinch-by-the-Inch:** Tell girls, "If you read one subject 15 minutes per week, and multiply that by 52 weeks you will have gained 13 hours' knowledge on that subject during the year. Multiply this by 10 years (13 hours x 10), and you have 130 hours of knowledge on the subject. Multiply this by 6 subjects (130 hours x 6) and you have 780 hours knowledge on your chosen subject. A college or trade school should be a cinch if you study <u>now</u> by the inch."

SUCCESS SNACKS: Jelly Bean Cupcakes. Place 2 jelly beans on top of cupcakes representing fiction and non-fiction books. Ask girls to say "fiction" or "non-fiction" as you read the book selections listed in Activity #1 above.

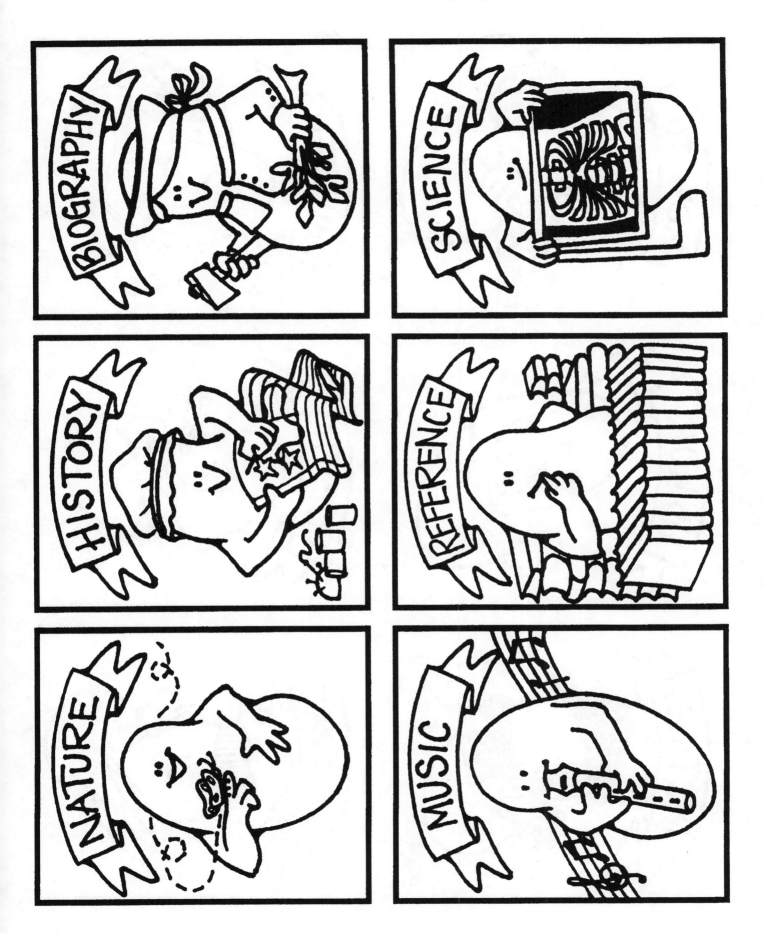

PATTERN: EDUCATION & SCHOLARSHIP invitations for Goal #1 and Goal #2 ♥ See pages 52 and 54 for details.

Family History: Goal #1

My Family Tree and Me:
Start a Family Group Sheet or Pedigree Chart

To:_____
Date:_____
Time:_____
Place:_____

Who's in your family tree?

YOU'LL NEED: Copies of invitation (page 65) on colored cardstock paper, My Family Tree and Me poster (pages 60-61), a Family Group sheet and/or Pedigree Chart for each girl, scissors, glue, washable markers, and Success Snacks.

INVITATIONS: Make and deliver a week ahead.

DO AHEAD: Talk to parents ahead of time to find out what records they have so girls can bring them. Goal is to help girls fill out a Family Group Sheet and Pedigree Chart.

CREATE A FAMILY TREE: Tell the girls that families are like trees. The branches grow as children are born into the family. When each child gets married and has children, branches grow. You are a branch of your mother and father's family tree. Your mother and father are branches of your grandparents' family tree. Let's create a family tree to see where your family tree started.

Activity #1 My Family Tree and Me Poster: Help girls color and cut out parts A and B and glue or tape together. Add names to the family tree (write out in pencil first). OPTION: Reduce pictures to size and place inside apple frames. Girls can laminate and mount poster on their wall.

Activity #2 Pedigree Chart: Tell girls that their family tree is their pedigree showing both their mother and father's side of their family. Show your own Pedigree Chart where you are listed on line number 1 and your father above and mother below with your parents and grandparents. Help them fill in their own Pedigree Chart with the information you have collected from their family.

Activity #3 Family Group Record: Show girls the Family Group Record to fill out for their father's and mother's immediate family where they can be listed with all the children. Help girls fill in their own personal Family Group Record.

SUCCESS SNACKS: **Broccoli Trees.** Steam broccoli and melt cheese on top. Talk about how strong a family can be if all the branches stick together, love and serve one another. Without family support, the branches thin out and lose their strength. Talk about ways they can support their family, i.e. family prayer, scripture reading, helping without being asked, doing special deeds without notice, complimenting, being positive, wearing a smile, making gifts and cards to cheer and show love.

Family Tree Fudge. ♥ Melt 2 (11.5 ounce) packages sweet milk chocolate chips in microwave one minute. ♥ Stir in 1 (14 ounce) can sweetened condensed milk and microwave 1 minute. ♥ Stir in vanilla and microwave 1 minute. Option: Add 2 cups miniature marshmallows and stir. Fudge thickens as it cools, so work fast. ♥ Shape fudge into top portion of tree and place on a serving plate. Press a brown wafer cookie into the bottom of fudge for tree trunk. Decorate tree by adding green colored coconut (leaves) and/or candy pieces to look like fruit. To color coconut, place 3/4 cup coconut in a plastic bag, add a few drops of green food coloring, close bag and mix.

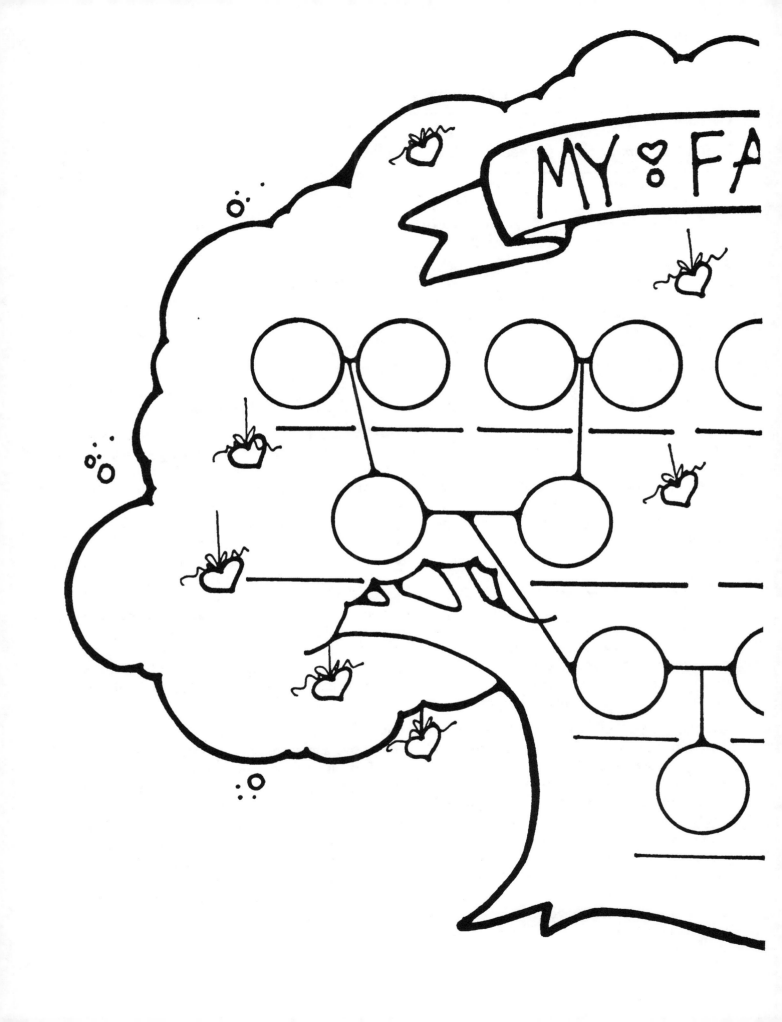

Family History: Goal #2

Journal Jazz!
Create a Journal and Book of Remembrance

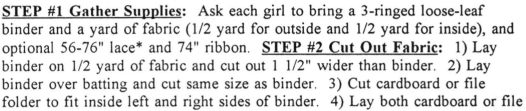

YOU'LL NEED: Copies of invitation (page 65) on colored cardstock paper, two copies each of My Journal and My Special Day (pages 63-64) for each girl, extra 3-ringed binders, fabric, enough batting to cover each girl's binder, cardboard or file folders, glue-gun and/or fabric or craft glue, pencils, crayons or washable markers, scissors, and Success Snacks.

INVITATIONS: Make & deliver ahead.

CREATE A NOTEBOOK COVER FOR BOOK OF REMEMBRANCE AND JOURNAL:

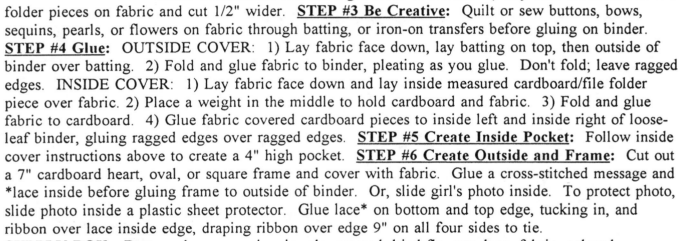

STEP #1 Gather Supplies: Ask each girl to bring a 3-ringed loose-leaf binder and a yard of fabric (1/2 yard for outside and 1/2 yard for inside), and optional 56-76" lace* and 74" ribbon. **STEP #2 Cut Out Fabric:** 1) Lay binder on 1/2 yard of fabric and cut out 1 1/2" wider than binder. 2) Lay binder over batting and cut same size as binder. 3) Cut cardboard or file folder to fit inside left and right sides of binder. 4) Lay both cardboard or file folder pieces on fabric and cut 1/2" wider. **STEP #3 Be Creative:** Quilt or sew buttons, bows, sequins, pearls, or flowers on fabric through batting, or iron-on transfers before gluing on binder. **STEP #4 Glue:** OUTSIDE COVER: 1) Lay fabric face down, lay batting on top, then outside of binder over batting. 2) Fold and glue fabric to binder, pleating as you glue. Don't fold; leave ragged edges. INSIDE COVER: 1) Lay fabric face down and lay inside measured cardboard/file folder piece over fabric. 2) Place a weight in the middle to hold cardboard and fabric. 3) Fold and glue fabric to cardboard. 4) Glue fabric covered cardboard pieces to inside left and inside right of loose-leaf binder, gluing ragged edges over ragged edges. **STEP #5 Create Inside Pocket:** Follow inside cover instructions above to create a 4" high pocket. **STEP #6 Create Outside and Frame:** Cut out a 7" cardboard heart, oval, or square frame and cover with fabric. Glue a cross-stitched message and *lace inside before gluing frame to outside of binder. Or, slide girl's photo inside. To protect photo, slide photo inside a plastic sheet protector. Glue lace* on bottom and top edge, tucking in, and ribbon over lace inside edge, draping ribbon over edge 9" on all four sides to tie.

SUPPLY BOX: Buttons, bows, sequins, jewels, pressed dried flowers, lace, fabric, colored construction and cardstock paper, stickers, pictures from magazines, cards, clip-art books, stencils, paints, markers (light/bright colors that don't color over images), lettering, rick-rack, plastic covers and paper (acid free best), spray-mount glue (for easy removal), rubber cement glue, colored pencils, cartoons, jokes, theater tickets, certificates, invitations, cards, awards, photographs, ruler, paper punches and scissors (different shapes), paper clips, file folders, and labels to organize.

JOURNAL PAGES: Give girls copies of My Journal and My Special Day pages to get started. Encourage girls to write a Family History starting with these journal pages.

JOURNAL JAZZ: Have girls and other adults who have completed attractive books show and tell about their books. Talk about how you can give your journal jazz! Example: Cut out cardstock paper to create letters and designs. Use imagination to create themes for each page, creative writing, poetry, and rhymes. Start a collection box of scrapbook crafts to design and decorate around photos and journal experiences.

SUCCESS SNACKS: Book of Remembrance Cake. Frost a 9" x 13" cake and use a decorator tube with contrasting frosting to write "Book of Remembrance" and "Journal" and waving lines. Place a photo in a plastic bag and place on cake, then place 3 licorice pieces in the center as binder rings.

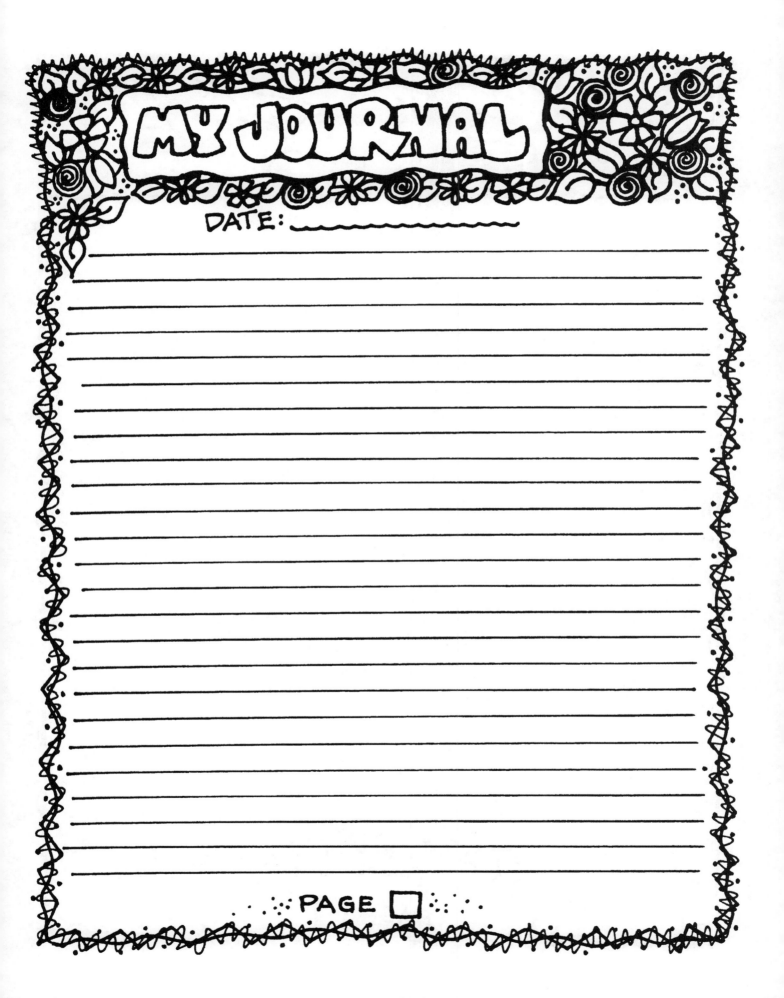

MY JOURNAL

DATE: _____

_____
_____
_____
_____
_____
_____
_____
_____
_____
_____
_____
_____
_____
_____
_____
_____
_____
_____
_____
_____
_____
_____
_____
_____
_____

PAGE ☐

MY SPECIAL DAY

PAGE ☐

PATTERN: FAMILY HISTORY invitations for Goal #1 and Goal #2 ♥ See pages 59 and 62 for details.

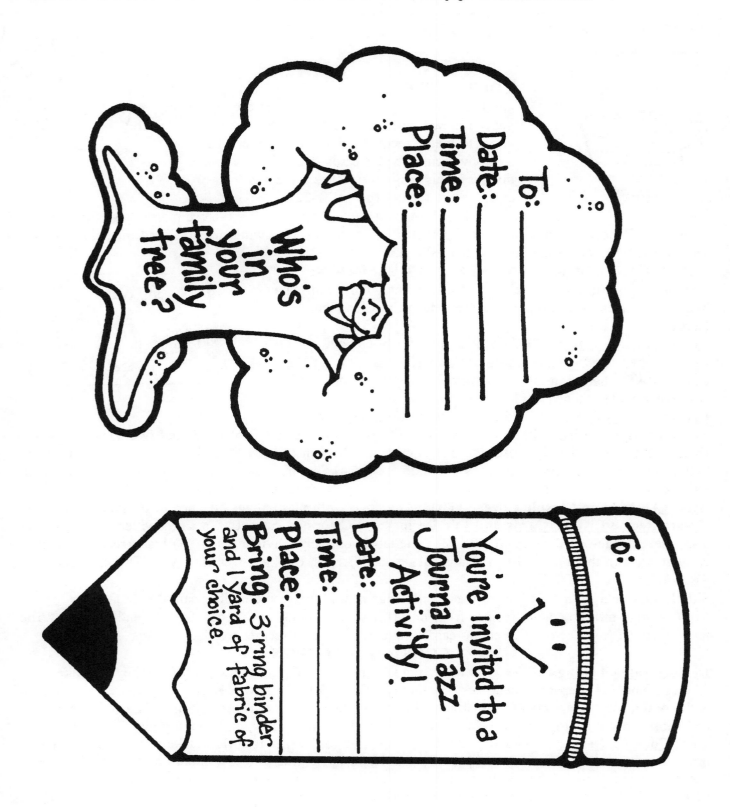

To:
Date:
Time:
Place:

Who's in your family tree?

To:

You're invited to a Journal Jazz Activity!

Date:
Time:
Place:
Bring: 3-ring binder and 1 yard of fabric of your choice.

Family Skills: Goal #1

I "Can" Cook! - *Create a delicious dinner*

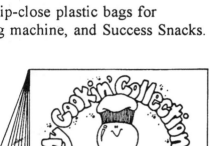

YOU'LL NEED: 1) Copies of invitation (page 79) and recipe book cover (page 67) on colored cardstock paper for each girl. 2) Sheet of colored cardstock paper to match recipe book cover for each girl. 3) Copy recipe divider cards (page 68), 10 recipe divider labels (page 69), 10 recipe cards (page 70), and 1 set of recipes (pages 71-72) for each girl. 4) 4. 10 (6 1/2" x 5 7/8") zip-close plastic bags for each girl. 5) Scissors, clear contact paper, stapler, sewing kit or sewing machine, and Success Snacks.
INVITATION: Make and deliver a week ahead.

I "CAN" COOK! MENU RECIPE COLLECTION:

Encourage girls to collect recipes and plan menus. Girls can make a book with plastic bags to insert recipes and recipes for menu plans. Here's How:

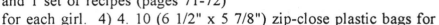

Create Outside Cover. 1) Color and cut out My Cookin' Collection: I "Can" Cook! recipe book cover (page 67). 2) Have each girl write her name on the book cover. 3) Laminate outside with clear contact paper.

Create Inside Cover. 1) Fold inside cover (matching colored cardstock paper) in half. 2) Lay five zip-close bags on the inside left of paper and five bags on inside right of paper with the zip-close side out, overlapping bottom of bags 1" in the center. 3) Pin or staple bottom left and right corners of bags to inside cover. 4) Sew bags to cover with a needle and thread or fishing line or sew zig-zag with a sewing machine. 5) Remove staples or pins.

Attach Outside and Inside Cover. Glue inside cover with plastic bags attached to outside cover.

Create Recipe Divider Cards and File Recipes. 1) Color and cut out 10 recipe divider cards (page 68) and 1 set of glue-on labels (page 69). 2) Glue labels on recipe divider cards. 3) Insert recipe divider cards in bags in this order: Menu Plans, Beverages, Breads, Cookies, Desserts, Main Dishes, Pasta and Rice, Salads, Side Dishes, and Soup. 4) File recipes inside bags behind the recipe divider cards.

5) Encourage girls to collect recipes from magazines, cookbooks, newspaper, friends, and family. Write the recipes on My Cookin' Collection cards (page 70) or attach recipes to 4" x 6" cards.

COOKING ACTIVITIES:

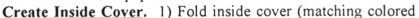

Demonstrate Cooking: Show girls how to create the four recipes (pages 71-72), so they can take recipes home and prepare a meal for their family. Once girls see how easy it is to prepare, they can cook with confidence. Share cooking tips from children's cookbooks, i.e. measuring liquids, dry ingredients, and shortening; cracking eggs carefully, stove, oven, and knife safety, and cooking tools.

Girls Cooking Demos: Photocopy and assign a variety of recipes to girls to take home and try. Then bring the recipe to Achievement Days with samples to try, giving girls the opportunity to show-and-tell about their creations. Schedule these in the weeks ahead and remind girls a week before.

SUCCESS SNACKS: **Marshmallow Chef Favor.** Attach two large marshmallows with two toothpicks. To make chef's hat, pull top marshmallow in with a string and tie. To make face, pull out marshmallow at eyes, nose, and mouth (to make sticky) and place candies for eyes, nose, mouth.

Four Course Meal Tasting Table. Use the four recipes on pages 71-72.

I can cook!
And not just from the
Learning how to cook is a piece
of. It's easy as
I just read the recipe
and give it a try!

My Cookin' Collection!

PATTERN: My Cookin' Collection recipe divider cards.
1. Copy 10 cards for each girl (to insert in zip-close plastic bags).
2. Glue on recipe divider labels (page 69): Menu Plan, Beverages, Breads, Cookies, Desserts, Main Dishes, Pasta and Rice, Salads, Side Dishes, and Soup.

PATTERN: My Cookin' Collection recipe divider labels ♥ Glue on recipe divider cards (page 68).

Menu Plans	**Beverages**
Breads	**Cookies**
Desserts	**Main Dishes**
Pasta and Rice	**Salads**
Side Dishes	**Soup**
Menu Plans	**Beverages**
Breads	**Cookies**
Desserts	**Main Dishes**
Pasta and Rice	**Salads**
Side Dishes	**Soup**

PATTERN: My Cookin' Collection recipe cards to place in zip-close bags behind recipe category cards filed A-Z
♥ Copy 4 cards on cardstock paper, and 1 pattern on lightweight paper for each girl.

_____'s Cookin' Collection:

_____'s Cookin' Collection:

PATTERN: Recipes to prepare a 4-course meal to serve a family of 5

_____'s Cookin' Collection:

Ham & Potato Soup
5 potatoes
6 ounces cooked ham
cubes
3 cups milk
2 tablespoons butter
1/4 teaspoon salt
1/8 teaspoon pepper
3/4 cup shredded cheddar cheese
Pour water into a medium size pan until it
is 3/4th full. Bring water to a boil on high
heat. While water is coming to a boil, wash potatoes. Place them in boiling
water with skins on. Boil 20 minutes or until you can pierce them with a fork
and they appear soft. Drain potatoes and run cold water over them. Let cool 10
minutes. Peel potatoes and chop into 1" squares. Place in medium size pan and
add milk. Warm milk slowly on medium heat, stirring often. Add ham, butter,
salt, pepper, and cheddar cheese. Simmer 5 minutes.

_____'s Cookin' Collection:

Baking Powder Biscuits
1/2 cup oil
1 cup milk
2 tablespoons water
2 tablespoons baking
powder
1 teaspoon salt
2 2/3 cup flour
Spray baking pan with cooking oil, or
grease with oil or butter. Preheat oven
to 425 degrees. Mix oil, milk, and
water in a large bowl. Mix baking
powder, salt, and flour in a separate bowl. Gradually add dry ingredients, mixing
until smooth. Roll dough 1/2" thick with a rolling pin. Cut out rolls with a 3"
biscuit cutter. Place rolls 1" apart on baking pan. Bake 15-16 minutes until
golden brown. Serve hot with honey butter (1/2 honey and 1/2 butter mixed),
butter, jam, or jelly. Makes 13 biscuits or rolls.

PATTERN: Recipes to prepare a 4-course meal to serve a family of 5

_____'s Cookin' Collection:

<u>Peachy-Keen</u>
<u>Fruit Salad</u>
2 (10-ounce) cans sliced
peaches
1 small can orange juice
concentrate (frozen)
1 small bottle maraschino
cherries
1 small carton whipped
topping

Drain juice from can of sliced peaches.
Place peaches in a medium size bowl. Drain juice from bottle of maraschino
cherries. Cut cherries in half and place in bowl with peaches. In a separate
medium size bowl, stir together orange juice concentrate and whipped topping.
Mix orange/whipped topping into peaches and cherries. OPTION: Slice and add
bananas.

_____'s Cookin' Collection:

<u>Pineapple Upside-Down Cake</u>
1 yellow cake mix
1/2 cup butter
1 cup packed brown sugar
1 (20-ounce) can
pineapple rings
10-15 maraschino cherries
Walnut halves

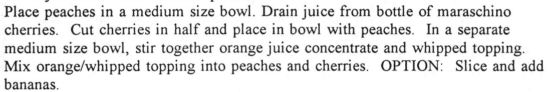

Heat oven to 350 degrees. Melt 1/2 cup
butter in a 13" x 9" x 2" rectangular pan in
350° oven until melted. Sprinkle 1 cup
packed brown sugar over melted butter. Place pineapple rings
(1 20-ounce can--drained) on top of butter/sugar mixture. Place maraschino
cherries in the center of each pineapple and walnut halves between pineapple
rings. Prepare yellow cake mix according to directions on package. Pour batter
into pan over pineapple rings. Bake 45-55 minutes. Within 5 minutes, turn over
on heatproof serving plate.

Family Skills: Goal #2

Super Sitter Basics - *Create a child care kit with care*

YOU'LL NEED the following for each girl: Copies of invitation, Animals Help Me, fish, fish bowl, and pole (pages 74-76, 79) on cardstock paper. Copies of Super Sitter Journal and Gratitude Gopher game (pages 77-78) on lightweight paper. Supplies: Zip-close plastic bags, scissors, double-stick tape, clear contact paper (to laminate) sticky-back Velcro, crayons or watercolor markers, and Success Snacks.

INVITATION: Make and deliver a week ahead.

SUPER SITTER IDEAS:

1. <u>Decorate a Super Sitter Box:</u> Encourage girls to cover a box with contact paper or fabric, cut out the I ♥ Babies invitation picture and glue on box. Add to box the following: Super Sitter Journal pages, books, children's magazines, toys, pen, play money (pattern on page 108, 110), coloring book and crayons, games, treats, playtime things, a bandaid box first aid kit (page 116), and fun activities.

2. <u>Create Children's Activities:</u> #1 <u>Animals Help Me</u> (page 74): Color poster and cards, laminate (using clear contact paper), and place sticky-back Velcro on back of cards and on poster squares. Tape a zip-close bag on back to store pieces Girls can help the children match squares with animals showing how animals help us with food, clothing, pets. Suggest girls share a box of animal crackers with children when they present this activity. #2 <u>Gratitude Gopher</u> match game (page 78). #3 <u>Fish and Water Animals: Fishy Fun</u> (pages 75-76): Color and cut out fish/water animals, bowl, pole, and hook. Attach plastic bag to back of fish bowl with double-stick tape and enclose fish/water animals. Attach a metal paper clip to each fish (so magnet fish hook can pull them out). Place fish in bag/fish bowl. Color and cut out fishing pole. Fold pattern in half and glue over wooden craft stick, poke a hole in end, and tie a string to pole. Tie fish hook to the other end of string. Glue a magnet on fish hook.

3. <u>Suggest Copy-and-Create Activity Ideas.</u> Some of these activities were taken from *Primary Partners: Nursery* activity book (see back of this book for details). You'll also find: 3-D Noah's ark, bird watch, bug jar, "NATURE WALK" binoculars, paper dolls, giant eyes headband, family tree, smile and frown flip-flag, fish, fish bowl, and fishing pole, finger puppets, friendship necklace, job-jar, garden bracelets, hippo sack puppet, and more.

4. <u>Share Super Sitter Safety Ideas:</u> See Stranger Danger (page 112), walk through a home to check for poison control, sharp or small objects, first-aid book, door locking, and fire drill. Remind girls to keep phone lines open for important calls, know if parents are expecting deliveries and calls and what to do, write down information or messages, know medications needed, where flashlight is, and emergency phone numbers, special instructions about the baby, and to never leave child alone.

5. <u>Suggest Other Fun Projects and Activities:</u> Making faces and objects with paper plates and colored paper, stenciling, collage, stamps, clay, jewelry, paper circus, felt objects and figures, puzzles, sewing cards, ring toss, mini masks, making a flip book, make music drums with pans and spoons, card table tents, indoor picnics, paper bag puppets, Old Maid and Go Fish card games, relay races, bubbles, store with play money, and more. Fun Treat: Sugar Babies® candy coated caramels, or Baby Ruth candy bars.

6. <u>Teach Girls Nursery Activities:</u> Ask a nursery leader to show the girls songs and activities.

7. <u>Show-and-Tell Baby:</u> Borrow a baby to demonstrate child care: Feeding, burping, changing diapers, talking to and playing with, holding, CPR, safety and emergency care.

SUPER SITTER SERVICE PROJECT: Give the girls a chance to test their Super Sitter skills by helping them tend children for a Relief Society social or other service project.

SUCCESS SNACKS: <u>Bottle Cookies.</u> Cut sugar cookie dough into baby bottle shapes, bake/frost.

ANIMALS
HELP ME

I am thankful for fish! ○ ○ I am thankful for fish! ○ ○ I am thankful for fish!

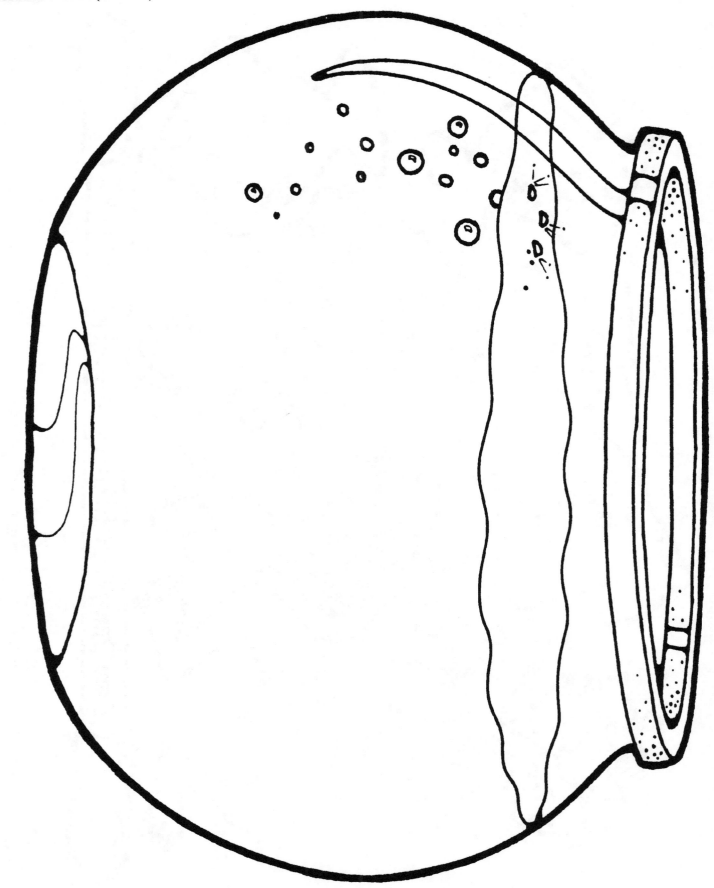

Super Sitter Journal

Parents _____
Address _____
Phone _____
Children:

♥   Age: ♥   Age:
♥   Age: ♥   Age:
♥   Age: ♥   Age:

EMERGENCY HELP:

Neighbor: Phone:
Doctor: Phone:
Fire & Police: 911
Parents located at _____ Phone _____
Parents will return at what time? _____

SPECIAL INSTRUCTIONS (food, bedtime, things to do):

Super Sitter Journal

Parents _____
Address _____
Phone _____
Children:

♥   Age: ♥   Age:
♥   Age: ♥   Age:
♥   Age: ♥   Age:

EMERGENCY HELP:

Neighbor: Phone:
Doctor: Phone:
Fire & Police: 911
Parents located at _____ Phone _____
Parents will return at what time? _____

SPECIAL INSTRUCTIONS (food, bedtime, things to do):

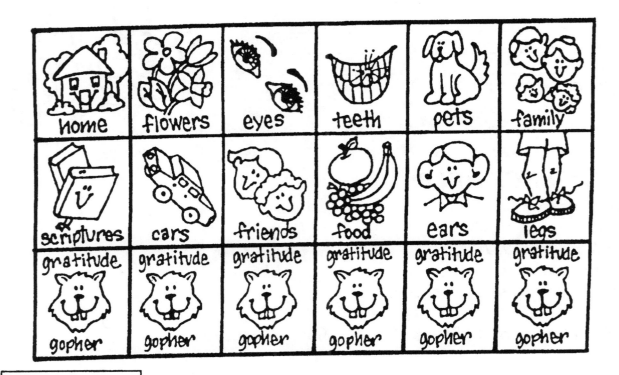

home	flowers	eyes	teeth	pets	family
scriptures	cars	friends	food	ears	legs
gratitude gopher	gratitude gopher	gratitude gopher	gratitude gopher	gratitude gopher	gratitude gopher

1) Color and cut out grab bag label and gratitude squares. 2) Paste grab bag label on small paper lunch sack or slip inside a zip-close plastic bag (to hold gratitude squares). 3) Place squares inside bag and play the **GAME:** Divide children into two teams on two sides of the room. Take turns, one child at a time, reaching into the bag and pulling out a gratitude square. As a child pulls out a gopher square have him or her tell one thing he or she is grateful for. **TO WIN:** Gratitude squares are worth one point and gopher squares are worth five points. The team with the most points wins!

GRATITUDE GOPHER GRAB BAG

PATTERN: FAMILY SKILLS invitations for Goal #1 and Goal #2 ♥ See pages 66 and 73 for details.

Health & Grooming: Goal #1

Apple-a-Day and Beauty Your Way
Start a health and beauty routine

YOU'LL NEED: Copies of invitation (page 89) and 2 sets Mega-Vitamin Match Game (pages 81-83) on colored cardstock paper, 2 My Apple-a-Day food and exercise diary, 2 Beauty Pinches routines, and Beauty Pinches success story (pages 84-85) for each girl, scissors, crayons or washable markers, and Success Snacks.

INVITATION: Make and deliver a week ahead. Punch a hole and tie curler on invitation with a pretty ribbon.

HEALTH Activity #1 My Apple-a-Day the Healthy Way Routine: Give each girl a cold, crisp, delicious apple to crunch as you begin. Remind the girls that *"An apple a day keeps the doctor away."* Here are the reasons it is important to eat an apple each day: Natural sugars give you an instant burst of energy; an ideal snack, it's 85% water, helps prevent heart disease, known as *"nature's toothbrush"* because it helps clean teeth and massage gums, calms the nerves, aids digestion, removes toxins. Eat it with the skin on! Give each girl two copies of the Apple-a-Day the Healthy Way food and exercise diary (page 81); one to use now and one to copy. The food servings on the chart are based on the Food Guide Pyramid designed by health experts. Write food eaten above and check servings below.

HEALTH Activity #2 MEGA-VITAMIN MATCH GAME:
1. Ahead of time color and cut out two sets of cards (pages 82-83).
2. Explain that vitamins help nourish our body. The letters on the card tell us which parts of our body vitamins nourish: S = Skin, H = Hair, E = Eyes, N = Nails, B = Bones and Blood.
3. TO PLAY: Divide girls into teams to sit across from each other.
4. Place vitamin-rich food cards in front of both teams face up. Explain that if leader yells out a vitamin, i.e. "Vitamin A!," the first girl to grab two matching food cards that contain that vitamin wins a point for their team. The first team to earn 21 points wins! OTHER OPTION: If leader calls out: "skin," "hair," "eyes," "nails," "bones," or "blood," girls grab two matching cards that contain the letters S, H, E, B, or Blood.

BEAUTY Activity #1: Beauty Pinches Success Story: Read the Beauty Pinches: Grooming Success Story (page 85), then talk about the story and have girls share personal experiences.

BEAUTY Activity #2: Beauty Pinches Beauty Routine: Talk about personal grooming and hygiene reviewing the chart (page 84) point by point. Allow girls to share beauty tips, then post the routine at home as a reminder. OPTION: Color and then laminate for durability.

BEAUTY Activity #3: Beauty Shop Surprise: Give girls a manicure, facial, and/or hairstyle.

SUCCESS SNACKS: Apple & Hand-some Nail Cookies. Roll out sugar cookie dough between sheets of waxed paper. Place hand on top of dough and cut out hand cookie shape. Place on cookie sheet with waxed paper. Place Smarties® or jelly bean candies on fingernails and bake 9-12 minutes at 350°. Sugar Cookie Dough. Mix: 1 cup (2 sticks) butter, 1 1/2 cup sugar, 3 eggs, 2 tsp. vanilla extract, 1 tsp. cream of tartar, 1 tsp. soda, 2 tsp. baking powder, 1/8th tsp. salt, and 4 cups flour.

My Apple-a-Day the Healthy Way

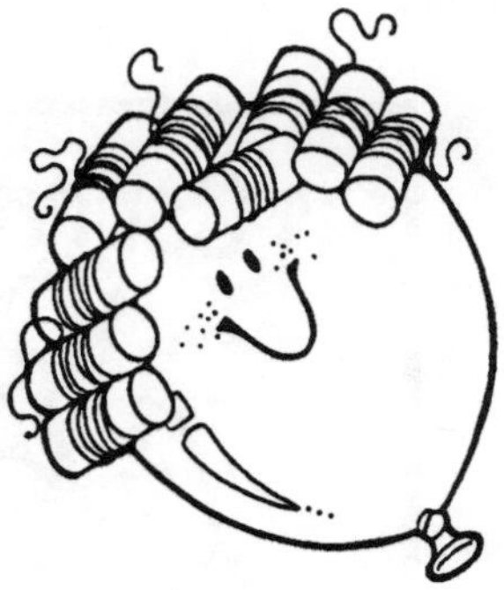

_____ 's Food and Exercise Diary:

♥ An **apple** is 85% water, high in fiber (nature's scrub brush), packed with vitamins, and claims to keep the doctor away.
♥ Vitamins A-E are in foods I eat and a multi-vitamin.
♥ I will try to balance each meal with basic food groups.
♥ I will try to drink 6-8 glasses water daily and eat natural sweets.

TODAY'S DATE: Exercise:

Breakfast: Dinner:

Lunch: Snacks:

Food Servings Check (below):   Water Check: A.M. ☐ ☐ - Noon ☐ ☐ - Afternoon ☐ ☐ - P.M. ☐ ☐

Milk ____ ____ ____ ____
Fats ____ ____
Fruit ____ ____ ____ ____
Vegetables ____ ____ ____ ____ ____

Protein ____ ____ ____
Bread ____ ____ ____ ____ ____ ____ ____
____ ____ ____ ____ ____
Sweets: Go for the natural sugars found in fruit. There are no vitamins in sugar.

TODAY'S DATE: Exercise:

Breakfast: Dinner:

Lunch: Snacks:

Food Servings Check (below):   Water Check: A.M. ☐ ☐ - Noon ☐ ☐ - Afternoon ☐ ☐ - P.M. ☐ ☐

Milk ____ ____ ____ ____
Fats ____ ____
Fruit ____ ____ ____ ____
Vegetables ____ ____ ____ ____ ____

Protein ____ ____ ____
Bread ____ ____ ____ ____ ____ ____ ____
____ ____ ____ ____ ____
Sweets: Go for the natural sugars found in fruit. There are no vitamins in sugar.

TODAY'S DATE: Exercise:

Breakfast: Dinner:

Lunch: Snacks:

Food Servings Check (below):   Water Check: A.M. ☐ ☐ - Noon ☐ ☐ - Afternoon ☐ ☐ - P.M. ☐ ☐

Milk ____ ____ ____ ____
Fats ____ ____
Fruit ____ ____ ____ ____
Vegetables ____ ____ ____ ____ ____

Protein ____ ____ ____
Bread ____ ____ ____ ____ ____ ____ ____
____ ____ ____ ____ ____
Sweets: Go for the natural sugars found in fruit. There are no vitamins in sugar.

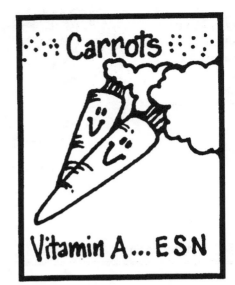

Carrots

Vitamin A...E S N

Broccoli

Vitamin B...B S H

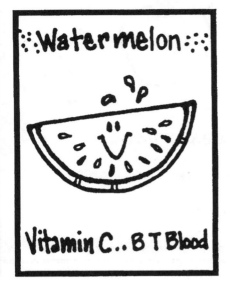

Watermelon

Vitamin C..B T Blood

Milk

Vitamin D ...BT

Bread

Vitamin E.. Blood

Leafy Greens

Vitamin K...Blood

Cantaloupe

Vitamin A...E S N

Fish

Vitamin B.. B S H

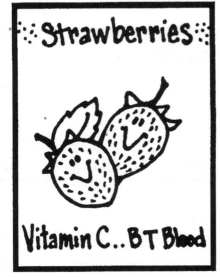

Strawberries

Vitamin C..BT Blood

Tuna Fish

Vitamin D.....B T

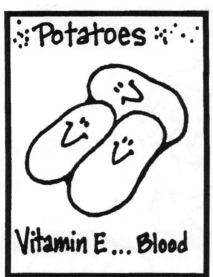

Potatoes

Vitamin E...Blood

Cereal

Vitamin K...Blood

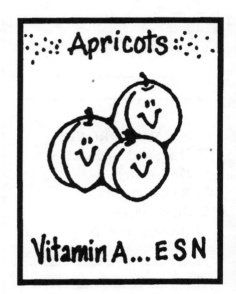

Apricots

Vitamin A...E S N

Peanut Butter

Vitamin B...B S H

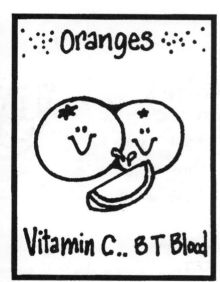

Oranges

Vitamin C.. B T Blood

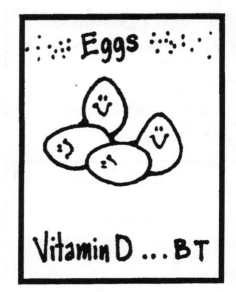

Eggs

Vitamin D ...B T

Sunflower Seeds

Vitamin E ...Blood

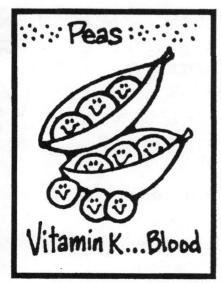

Peas

Vitamin K...Blood

BEAUTY PINCHES!

A little bit more time and effort is needed to look my best.

DAILY PLAN:

SKIN:
- ☐ Bathe body
- ☐ Wash ears
- ☐ Wash face
- ☐ Lotion

HAIR:
- ☐ Wash
- ☐ Condition
- ☐ Style

MOUTH & TEETH:
- ☐ Brush 3 x day
- ☐ Floss
- ☐ Brush tongue

HANDS & FEET:
- ☐ File nails
- ☐ Lotion

CLOTHES & SHOES:
- ☐ Ready for next day ... the night before

EARLY RISE:
- ☐ Alarm Clock

(allow enough time to get ready and eat a healthy breakfast)

WEEKLY PLAN:

NAILS:
- ☐ Clean
- ☐ File
- ☐ Polish

WARDROBE:
- ☐ Hang and fold clothes
- ☐ Do laundry
- ☐ Repair clothes
- ☐ Shine shoes
- ☐ Drawers and shelves neat

ACCESSORIES:
Put Away, Clean and Repair:
- ☐ Shoes
- ☐ Belts
- ☐ Hair bows/barrettes
- ☐ Socks

SHOPPING:
- ☐ List grooming products and clothing needed
- ☐ Save money and purchase items needed

BEAUTY PINCHES
- A Personal Grooming Success Story -

"BEAUTY PINCHES" some say. Inner and outer beauty needs a little bit of time and effort, but it's worth it. Let's learn why.

♥ Anna, at age 8-10 complained when her mother shampooed her hair, especially when soap got in her eyes. Her mother said, "BEAUTY PINCHES."

♥ When her mother combed her hair and the comb caught in tangles, she cried. Mother gently said, "BEAUTY PINCHES."

♥ Anna complained when she had to floss and brush her teeth. Her mother said, "BEAUTY PINCHES."

♥ When it was time to wash her face, she would hear, "BEAUTY PINCHES."

"BEAUTY PINCHES ... What does this mean?" Anna would ask. Her mother and father would reply, "It means you have to work at staying healthy and beautiful. Sometimes it's a pain to wash your hair every day, groom yourself, take care of your clothes, take the time to fix vegetables or fruit instead of eating a cookie or candy. But the rewards are great. You will see."

As the years went by, Anna became more beautiful each day. Her hair shone and had a freshly-shampooed smell. Her posture was straight as she held her head high. You could tell her eating habits were healthy as she had a great amount of energy. Anna did well in school and made many friends.

The Rewards of a "BEAUTY PINCHES" Routine

When Anna lacked the energy to groom and eat right she would say to herself, "BEAUTY PINCHES." This gave her the push to pursue her goal to groom herself the best that she could each day. She tried to exercise and eat right. This gave her more energy.

But most of all she tried to smile. Her mother said she could go a mile with a smile. This meant that if she wanted to have friends, she would need to act happy. She realized that beauty is more than skin deep ... it's an inner feeling that radiates in a smile.

Anna is age 11 now and is an Achievement Days girl. Will she continue to push her way towards inner and outer beauty ... smiling as she remembers that "BEAUTY PINCHES"?

If you were Anna, what would you do?

Would you wait for someone like your mother or father to remind you? Or would you eat and groom each day the right way? Try These BEAUTY PINCHING Ideas:

♥ Wash your body daily

♥ Wash and style hair

♥ Eat a good breakfast

♥ Floss and brush teeth and tongue

♥ Drink lots of water and eat right

♥ Exercise to strengthen muscles

♥ Keep clothes clean and orderly

♥ _____

♥ _____

♥ _____

Health & Grooming: Goal #2

Closet Class! - *Organize room and wardrobe*

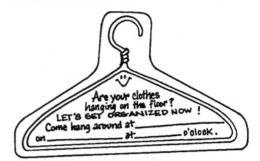

YOU'LL NEED: Copies of invitation (page 89) on colored cardstock paper, Sloppy Sal story, 2 copies of Closet Class! (pages 87-88) for each girl, washable markers, and Success Snacks.
INVITATION: Make and deliver a week ahead. FUN OPTION: Sew a button on invitation to decorate.
CREATE A CLASSY CLOSET: Color and read with girls the story of Sloppy Sal and talk about goals for a clean room and classy closet. Read the Closet Class! form and talk about hanging up clothes and creating an orderly closet. Show girls how a basic wardrobe is put together based on the information on the Closet Class form showing staple colors coordinating with boosters #1 and #2.

#1 CLOSET INSPECTION: Show your closet first to show how closet can be organized (see Closet Class! form (page 88). Then visit each girl's closet with the other girls to discover how they organize. Invitation asks girls to get their closet in order to show others how they organize their clothing and room. This is optional; they may or may not choose to show-and-tell.

#2 IRONING LESSON: Pull out items girls can iron, and give them a lesson on iron safety and technique. Tell girls that if they will take their laundry out of the dryer as soon as it is complete and hang up their clothes, they won't need to press most items. Demonstrate spray starch on shirts, ironing the collar first, then the yolk, sleeves, and body of shirt.

#3 SHOE SHINE KIT: Show girls how to polish, brush, and shine shoes. You may want to sew up a draw string cotton bag girls can take home. Demonstrate how to clean and care for dress and sports shoes. Encourage girls to keep shoes clean and change shoelaces. Encourage girls to put fun laces and even ribbons in shoes.

#4 ORDERLY DRESSER DRAWERS: Encourage girls to keep their dresser drawers orderly by using boxes to organize and adding sachets to lingerie (underwear) drawers. Fun Idea: Make sachets to place in dresser drawers, and/or line drawers with wrapping paper or drawer liners.

#5 DRESS-UP RELAY: Collect three girls' dress-up clothing items and place them in two different boxes 10 feet away from girls (who are divided into teams). At "go" first girls in the line race to the dress-up box and put on every item in the box, run to their team, model clothing by turning round once, and return to box, taking off dress-up items. *PRIZE: Award winning team with a licorice shoe lace.

#6 BUDGET CLOTHING FIELD TRIP: Take girls to a second-hand clothing store and challenge them to choose one or two matching outfits, including accessories. They can make note of items they want to return and purchase. This trip will encourage the girls to get in the habit of frugal shopping. More Ideas: Girls can bring clothing items they want to trade with each other, or sell at garage-sale prices.

SUCCESS SNACKS: <u>Button Cookies</u>. Divide sugar cookie dough into two parts (recipe page 80). Mix blue food coloring in one part and red in the other. Roll into 2" balls and press on a cookie sheet to bake. Place two M&M® candies or chocolate chips in center for button holes. Bake at 350° 8-10 minutes. Remind girls to button the top button of clothing after placing them on the hanger.

Will Sloppy Sal Lose Her Pal?

- A Personal Grooming Success Story -

Sal had a pal, a pen pal that is. Kimberly was a girl her aunt asked her to write to. Her letters were great. Kim wrote often and told Sal about the great time she had in the city, rollerblading in the park and swimming at the nearby pool. Sal wrote of the great time she had in the country horseback riding and swimming in the nearby pond.

Then one day Sal received a surprise visit from her friend whom she had never seen before. Kimberly was pretty. Her clothes were clean and her hair sparkled like her smile. "Kim, is that you?" "Yes Sal, it's me, pal!" Sal invited her in, and after lunch they decided to go for a swim.

Sal rushed in her room to find her polka dot suit. She was hoping that the bright dots would pop out at her as she searched through the pile of clothes on her floor, but it was nowhere! Just then Kim came in, and dropped her smiling grin when she saw Sal's room. Her eyebrows lifted, and her jaw dropped as she saw the place ... it needed a mop. A clean sweep, she thought as she started to stare.

"Oh, Sal! You're never a bore! But your room, it's, it's, well, it's ... can I help you?" Sal was totally embarrassed. Kim came so soon, Sal didn't have time to clean her room or groom. Sal's hair was tosseled from the night before, and her clothes were piled so thick you couldn't see the floor. Well, you can imagine. Her clothes looked like they were allergic to hangers, and her shoes were scattered and dresser drawers were open to the clutter.

"I guess we can't swim, as you can see the shape my room is in. "Let's go horseback riding instead."

When Sal finally found her best outfit, she noticed a big orange stain from last week's climb in the apricot tree. She had forgotten to put it in the laundry. She looked for her next best outfit; she found the top, but the shorts were lost. Sal finally found something to wear, but the button was missing. Looking for a sewing kit, she finally found a safety pin. She pinned the blouse and they were on their way. Just as Sal threw her arms up to get on the horse, the pin popped off her shirt and Kim looked at her strangely. Sal pinned it again and they went on. Sal was very uncomfortable when Kim walked off saying, "I care about you, but you haven't a thing to wear."

Kimberly left town soon with no more comments about Sal's room. Sal was worried that she had lost her pal Kim, knowing the fix she was in. But Kim was a good friend. She wrote her a nice letter in hopes that the next time she came, Sal would be a little more organized.

The letter read: "Dear Sal: It was nice to finally meet you and see where you live. I want to come again and to be your friend. I noticed that you were a bit jittery while I was there, so I thought I'd take the time to share some things my mother told me. When she was in college, she had a messy room. Her roommate Sandra was neat as a pin. She said, 'Let's dig in. The idea is to have a place for everything. Then it's easy to put everything in its place. When you are through wearing something, put it on a hanger or fold it neatly in your drawer; never on the bed or floor.' I hope this helps. Your friend, Kim."

Sal began to change. She decided to rearrange her room, and her looks. She really tried to keep her room clean, having a place for everything and everything in its place.

Kim came again, and what a great time they had from beginning to end. Sal knew right were to look for her polka dot swim suit, her best riding outfit, and she even knew where her sewing kit was in case a button happened to be missing. Kim invited her to visit her in the city next time. Sal could imagine what Kim's room must look like. Kim always looked so fresh when and well-groomed.

When Sal and Kim went to college they were roommates, and got along great!

The message in this story is: HOW YOU KEEP YOUR ROOM SHOWS HOW YOU GROOM or ... HOW YOU GROOM SHOWS HOW YOU KEEP YOUR ROOM.

How will your story turn out?

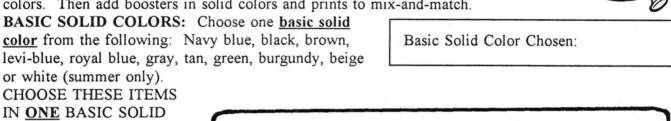

CLOSET CLASS!

I can plan my closet to create some class!

1. Dejunk: Pull out hangers not in use and place in a box or shelf.
2. Hang up every item by color or by items (all T-shirts together).
3. Ask yourself with each item: Is it clean, pressed, any buttons missing, do I like it and will I wear it?
4. Stretch your wardrobe. Add clothing items starting with basic solid colors. Then add boosters in solid colors and prints to mix-and-match.

BASIC SOLID COLORS: Choose one **basic solid color** from the following: Navy blue, black, brown, levi-blue, royal blue, gray, tan, green, burgundy, beige or white (summer only).

CHOOSE THESE ITEMS IN **ONE** BASIC SOLID

Basic Solid Color Chosen:

COLOR: ☐ T-shirt
☐ Socks   ☐ Shoes
☐ Blouse or knit shirt
☐ Pants   ☐ Skirt
☐ Jumper   ☐ Vest
☐ Belt   ☐ Coat
☐ Hair accessories

♥ Now stretch your wardrobe with boosters. Boosters add color and variety to your outfits.

♥ Here's how to add boosters #1 and #2 to the staple colors to create closet class!

Booster #1 Choose one or more **bright or light solid colors** in items listed above. Colors might be bright yellow or hot pink, or light colors like white or beige or light blue.

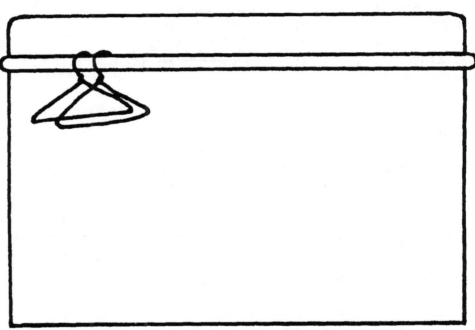

DRAWING OF MY ORGANIZED CLOSET

Booster #1 Solid Colors Chosen: _____
_____

Booster #2 Choose one or more **multi-colored prints** in items listed above. Make sure that your basic staple color and booster #1 solid bright or light color is in this print. Example: Wear navy blue pants with a yellow T-shirt, and a navy blue and yellow print vest. Prints can be plaids, flowers, dotted, or design.

Booster #2 Prints Chosen: _____
_____

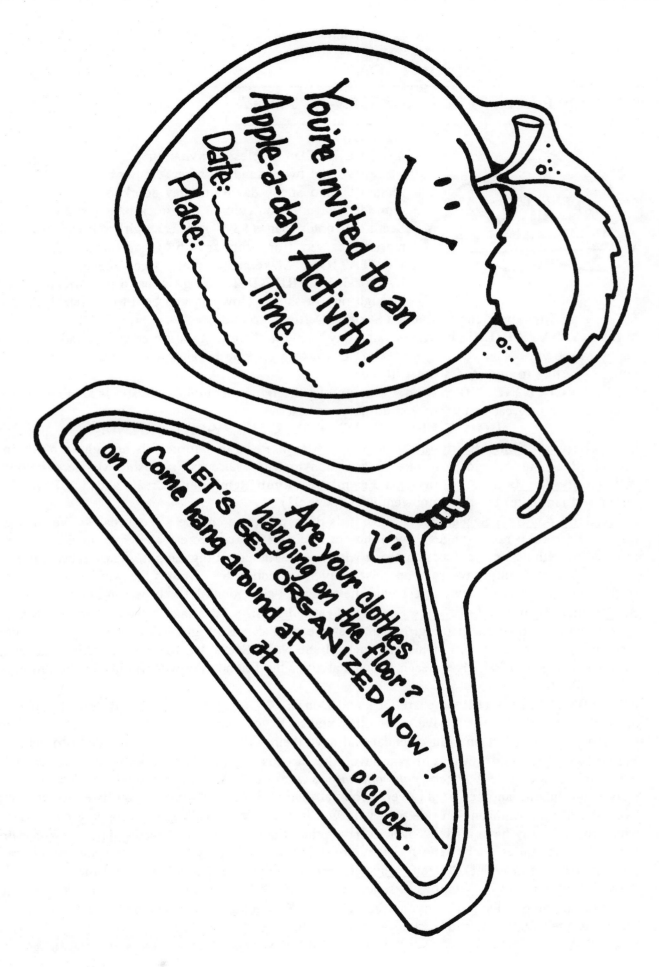

You're invited to an
Apple-a-day Activity!

Date: _____

Place: _____ Time: _____

Are your clothes
hanging on the floor?
LET'S GET ORGANIZED NOW!
Come hang around at _____
on _____ at _____ o'clock.

Hospitality: Goal #1

Friends Forever! - *Become a Rainy-day Friend*

YOU'LL NEED: Copies of invitation (page 98), and two Friends Forever! frames* (page 91), and Sunny-day/Rainy-day doorknob reminder (page 92) on colored cardstock paper, and one set of Secret Pal notes (pages 93-94) for each girl, scissors, washable markers, camera (for future activity*), and Success Snacks.

INVITATION: Make and deliver a week ahead.

RAINY-DAY FRIENDS: Tell girls that a true friend is kind through rain or shine. How can you be a true friend? A true friend is a rainy-day friend first and a sunny-day friend second.

♥ **RAINY-DAY FRIEND First:** A rainy-day friend is there in good times and in bad. They are happy to see you when you are not feeling or looking your best. They want to help you and cheer you. They like to give and share with you.

♥ **SUNNY-DAY FRIEND Second:** A sunny-day friend is there when the sun is shining--when things are going great and when you are at your best.

HOW TO BE A RAINY-DAY & SUNNY-DAY FRIEND:

▣ **Activity #1 Share Rainy-day Friendship Ideas:** Place invitation girls brought in a pile in front of you. Read the three ideas from each girl anonymously. Discuss Friendship Manners (below).

▣ **Activity #2 Rainy & Sunny-Day Friend Doorknob Reminder:** Create ahead a favor for girls (color and laminate) the doorknob reminder (page 92).

▣ **Activity #3 Be a Secret Pal:** Have girls draw names to choose a secret pal. Give each girl a set of 8 Secret Pal notes (pages 93-94) they can deliver to their secret pal. Give them several weeks to leave something on the doorstep along with note, without getting caught. They can doorbell ditch (ring the bell and run), have someone else deliver, or mail notes. Mum's the word ... this is secret stuff! Tell girls that if they suspect who their Secret Pal is, don't let that person know you know.

▣ ***Future Activity #4 Friends Forever! Framed Photo:** At a later activity when the Secret Pal is revealed, take pictures of the girls with their Secret Pals. Each girl can have two photos taken and make a frame for each: 1) For her and the girl she was a Secret Pal to, and 2) For her and the girl who was her Secret Pal. Have each Secret Pal color the Friends Forever! frame for the girl she was a Secret Pal to.

FRIENDSHIP MANNERS: Share Do's and Don'ts. ♥ <u>Do learn to say "no" if you can't play</u>. If they ask why, tell them you have made other plans. If you want to see them soon, schedule a time you can play. Write it on your calendar and have them write it on theirs ... and don't forget.

♥ <u>Don't say "yes" you can play</u> if you have other friends over, unless you know they know each other and get along: *"Two's company and three's a crowd."* Ask the friend who is there if they feel okay about having another friend over. Look at their facial expressions as you listen to their answer. Your friend may want one-on-one time with you instead. ♥ <u>Do call before dropping by</u>. Your friend may already have a friend over or have other plans. ♥ <u>Do call ahead a day or two</u> for Friday night play. It makes your friend feel they are important. Saturday play can be spontaneous; call them spur-of-the moment. ♥ <u>Don't whisper</u>. Friends think you are talking about them.

♥ <u>Don't give out party invitations</u> at school or church. ♥ <u>Don't brag</u> about yourself. ♥ <u>Do include</u> everyone in games. <u>Don't</u> let anyone feel left out. ♥ <u>Don't avoid</u> the un-smart or un-attractive. They are often your best and trusted friends--and need your friendship.

SUCCESS SNACKS: <u>Rainy-Day Lemonade and Sunny-Day Muffins</u> (make straw/toothpick signs)

PATTERN: Friend's Forever! frames to frame photos of Secret Pal . . . . HOSPITALITY

PATTERN: Rainy &
Sunny-Day Friend
doorknob reminder

You can really sparkle and shine!

Won't you be a friend of mine?

You're like a tube of toothpaste...

You give style to a smile!

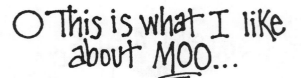

You're so appealing!

This is what I like about MOO...

○ Have a hoppy day!
3 Wishes for you:
1. _____
2. _____
3. No warts to wear on Sunday!

○ I'm grape-ful I know you!

○ If you ever need to cry...
You know who is close by! Call me!

○ I hope you have a bubbly fun day today!

Hospitality: Goal #2

Let's Be Pen Pals - *Create friends through Letters*

YOU'LL NEED: Copies of invitation (page 98) on colored cardstock paper, and Pen Pal stationery (pages 96-97) for each girl, scissors, glue, washable markers, and Success Snacks.

INVITATION: Make and deliver a week ahead.

WRITE LETTERS TO MAKE FRIENDS: Start by giving girls a fun favor to motivate letter writing: Make a carrot with a 5" x 8" piece of gold or orange cellophane or tissue paper filled with cheese flavored baked corn puffs and candy corns or jelly beans. Tape paper carrot together and fill with munchies. Tie with a bright green ribbon, metallic paper twist, or jute (rope string). Copy note pattern on page 96 and tie on carrot favor. Note reads:

"IF YOU CAR-ROT ALL ... WRITE ME A LETTER. - Your Pen Pal."

Ask girls to write 3 pen pal letters before they eat what's inside. Girls can exchange addresses or coordinate pen pals with other Achievement Days girls nearby; where they can join you for activities, meet and make new friends.

STATIONERY STARTERS: Tell girls that these are some ideas to start your letters with style! Design your own stationery with finesse by using your imagination. Start with the paper; use newspaper as a fun boarder by cutting plain paper smaller and gluing it on top. Design your stationary to fit the person you are writing to reflect that person's interests. Examples: If writing to someone who likes horses, draw horse shoes on the stationery. If your pen pal takes piano lessons, add a note with your note. Glue on pictures and stickers to create your own special stationery. Or, copy and use the stationery patterns (pages 96-97).

STATIONERY SUPPLIES: Colored paper, colored markers, pencils, crayons, stickers, stamps, stamp pads, glitter, ruler, pens, pencils, felt-tip pen, buttons to glue on, sacks, padding, twine or string, yarn, ribbon, paper punches and scissors of different shapes, idea books, i.e. pop-up cards and clip-art, photos of yourself to exchange, scratch paper, writing pad with lines, fabric scraps, magazines (to clip out pictures), envelopes, and postage stamps

LETTER WRITING IDEAS: Talk to the girls about letter writing ideas. ♥ Create an address book with pen pals and family. ♥ Write a letter within a week of someone's writing you. Be the first to write the letter. ♥ Keep the letter in sight until you have answered it. ♥ Design your stationery ahead of time so that when a letter arrives you can write back immediately. ♥ Plan ahead to buy stationery supplies. ♥ Write about your pen pal's interests and include some of your own. ♥ Send photographs asking your friend to send you a current snapshot. ♥ Begin collecting letters and photos in a scrapbook. ♥ Send your friend a card with a letter written on the card or slipped inside.   Homemade cards and stationery are more fun to receive. ♥ Visit the greeting card store for ideas, write them down, and let your imagination soar! ♥ Remember that a letter really warms the heart. It doesn't have to be long. It's the thought that counts, and your thoughts are always welcome to your pen pal.

SUCCESS SNACK: <u>Idea #1: Letter with Heart Treats</u>. Write a letter to each girl expressing what you like about her and that you are happy she is part of your group. Fill the letter with heart shaped or any shaped treats, signing the letter "Love, Your Achievement Days Leader."

<u>Idea #2: Licorice Treat</u>. Place licorice in a bag. Copy note (page 96) and attach to bag. Note reads: **"With this <u>licorice</u> treat, think about <u>licking</u> the habit of not writing letters. 1. Write the letter. 2. <u>Lick</u> the envelope. 3. <u>Lick</u> the stamp."**

Outdoor Fun & Skills: Goal #1

> ## Ladybug Gardening - Indoor/Outdoor Fun!
> *Create and decorate a window garden*

YOU'LL NEED:
Copies of invitation (page 104), pot perkers (page 100), and Where Have All

the Flowers Gone? cards (page 101) on colored cardstock paper, a 6" pot, and two 1/4" x 10" wooden dowels* for each girl, potting soil, seeds, gravel, clear contact paper (to laminate decorations), scissors, washable markers, decoupage paint, sponge brushes, acrylic tole paints, brushes, sponges, glue, and Success Snacks.

INVITATION: Make and deliver a week ahead.

CREATE A WINDOW GARDEN (great Mother's Day or friendship gift): <u>Decorate Pot</u>. Girls can write or glue the message (right) on their pot and surround it with flowers. Sponge-paint pot with acrylic paints. Cut sponges 1" square and dip into colors to paint rim. Sponge paint bottom of pot with white if flower background is white. Cut out flowers from wrapping paper, seed catalogs or magazines and glue on pot. Paint two coats of decoupage glaze over flowers to give glassy appearance. <u>Plant Flower Seeds</u>. Place gravel in bottom of pot and fill 1/2 full of potting soil, drop in seeds, fill to top and water. <u>Make Pot Perkers</u>. Color pot perker decorations (page 100). Cover with contact paper, punch holes and slip a 10" wooden dowel through holes and stick in pot. *OPTION: Use straws or wooden skewers in place of wooden dowels.

HERBS TO PLANT: Basil, oregano, marjoram, parsley, mint, rosemary, thyme, and chives. These herbs season our food. Fresh is best.

LADYBUG GARDENING TIPS:

1. Talk about ladybugs, a small red beetle with black spots. They help us by ridding our garden of aphids and pesky insects.

2. Visit a garden center or gardening expert's yard for advice on gardening.

3. Check out a few simple gardening books at the library, clip gardening tips from the newspaper and magazines to show girls how to get started collecting gardening tips.

Hide-and-Seek--Where Have All the Flowers Gone?: Girls color and cut out a set of flower cards (page 101) and hide cards in assigned rooms. Girls divide into two teams and at "GO" rush to find hidden flowers, and trade flowers for a complete set to paste in their Nature Lover's Scrapbook (see page 102). If girls want to keep the flowers they colored, place initials on back. Award winning team with an extra treat or flower from your garden. Decorate Nature Lover's Scrapbook with flower cards (see page 102).

SUCCESS SNACKS--GARDEN TREATS: Treat #1--<u>Ladybug Cookies</u>. Make sugar cookie dough (recipe page 80) and color with red food coloring. Roll dough into 1 1/2" oval balls. Place on pan and press top with 5 chocolate chip spots and black gumdrop (or chocolate chip) head.

Treat #2--<u>Flower Garden Cupcakes</u>. Mix and bake cupcakes (below). Frost with chocolate frosting and top with gumdrop worms and flowers. Worms: Press small white gumdrops with rolling pin and cut in half and piece together (option: purchase gummy worms). Flowers: Press small red, yellow, or purple gumdrops with rolling pin into round shapes and cut edges with knife to create petals. Press green gumdrops into rectangle shapes and cut in half lengthwise for leaves. Slice yellow or orange gumdrop for flower centers. Push a toothpick through flower parts.

GARDEN CUPCAKE RECIPE: 3/4 cup oil, 1 cup sugar, 3 eggs (cream together). Add 2 cups flour, 2 teaspoons baking powder, 1 1/2 teaspoon soda, and 1/2 teaspoon salt. Add 2 cups zucchini and 1 cup grated carrots, and 1/2 cup chopped nuts. Fill cupcake liners three-fourths full. Bake at 350° for 22 minutes (makes 24).

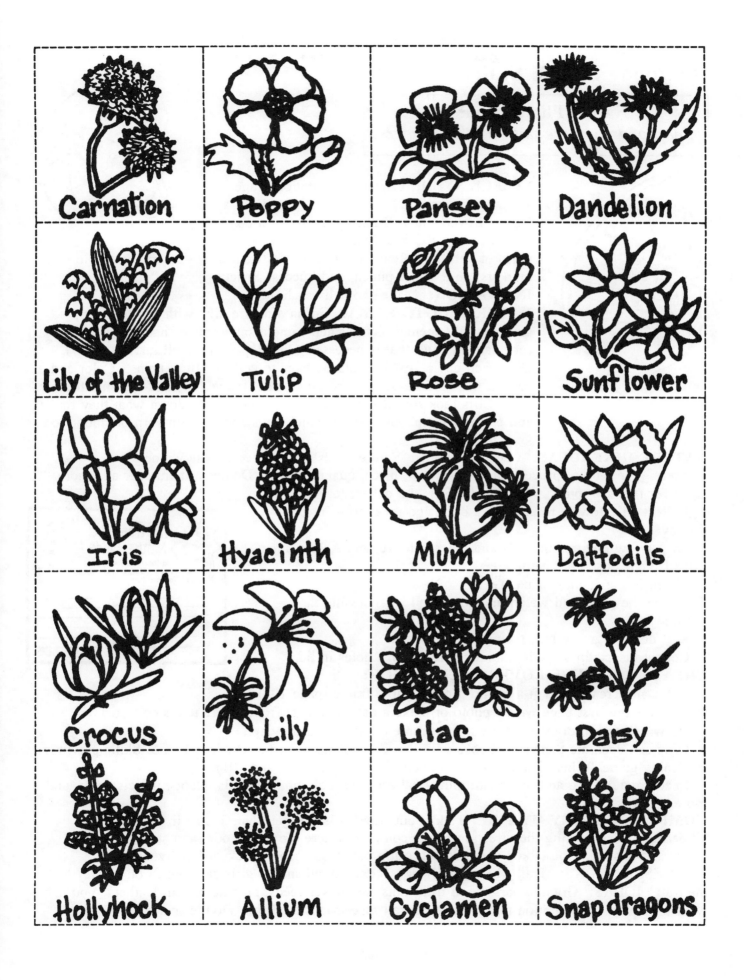

Carnation

Poppy

Pansey

Dandelion

Lily of the Valley

Tulip

Rose

Sunflower

Iris

Hyacinth

Mum

Daffodils

Crocus

Lily

Lilac

Daisy

Hollyhock

Allium

Cyclamen

Snapdragons

Outdoor Fun & Skills: Goal #2

> ## Nature Photo-rama!
> *Snap and compare nature hike wonders*

YOU'LL NEED: Copies of invitation (page 104), 12 Tree-rific Nature Finds! list and I'm a Nature Lover! photo frame (page 103) on colored cardstock paper, 7 zip-close plastic bags, and 6" piece of yarn or ribbon, and a pencil for each girl, scissors, washable markers, glue, paper punch, and Success Snacks.

INVITATION: Make and deliver ahead.

NATURE PHOTO-RAMA: Go on a nature hike with adults to help so girls can take mental pictures and camera snapshots of nature's wonders (one camera is all that is necessary--develop film for all girls to enjoy). Give each girl 6 zip-close plastic bags to collect nature items. Color and cut out the 12 Tree-ific Nature Finds label (page 103) and slip into the first bag. Girls look for 12 items to place in bags, write down what they found and paste in scrapbook. Paper punch bags and tie with yarn or ribbon to keep together.

NATURE HIKE IDEAS: Use 12 Tree-rific Nature Finds! list to record observations.

1. Trees: Pine, blue spruce, oak, ash, willow, birch, quaking aspen, Douglas fir, juniper and more. Look for tree sap, pick up bark and twigs, and collect leaves.
2. Collect wildflowers to press in a book and rocks to paint or display.
3. Snap a few pictures of birds and other wildlife, and Achievement Days friends observing nature.
4. Listen to the sounds of nature.
5. Lie on the grass and watch the clouds roll by, guessing their shapes.
6. Roll down a grassy hill, racing to the bottom.
7. Collect insects in a bottle, making sure to poke holes in lid.

CREATE A NATURE LOVER'S SCRAPBOOK:

1. Color and create the I'm a Nature Lover! photo frame (page 103) to decorate the first page with a photo or make a nature collage from nature items collected. If photo wasn't taken, draw a picture inside frame to remember the day.
2. Girls can decorate their scrapbooks with flower cards used for the Outdoor Fun & Skills previous gardening game "Where Have All the Flowers Gone?" (pages 99 and 101).
3. Encourage girls to add information they collect at school about animals, plants, insects, trees, and more.

COMPASS AND SKY WATCH: Talk about ways girls can get home if lost in the forest or wilderness, i.e. watching the direction of the compass, where the sun, moon, and stars are located. Survival skills could be talked about as you camp out in someone's backyard or living room.

SUCCESS SNACKS: Trail Mix Super Snacks. Pack dried snacks girls can munch on as they hit the trail. IDEAS: Granola bars, dried fruit, nuts, sunflower seeds, pine nuts, fruit leather. You may want to request on invitation that girls bring trail mix snacks to share. Divide snacks into bags.

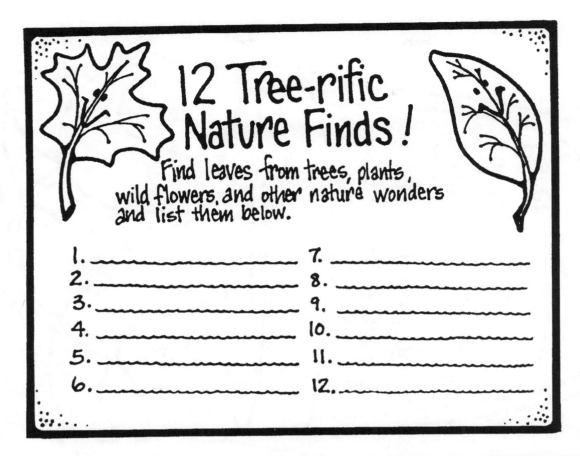

12 Tree-rific Nature Finds!

Find leaves from trees, plants, wild flowers, and other nature wonders and list them below.

1. _____   7. _____
2. _____   8. _____
3. _____   9. _____
4. _____   10. _____
5. _____   11. _____
6. _____   12. _____

I'm a NATURE LOVER!

Cut Out

PATTERN: OUTDOOR FUN & SKILLS invitations for Goal #1 and Goal #2 ♥ See pages 99 and 102 for details.

You're invited to come be a Ladybug Gardener!

Date: _____
Time: _____
Place: _____

Hey, Nature Lover! You're invited to the great outdoors!

Date: _____
Time: _____
Place: _____
Don't be leafed out!

Personal Preparedness: Goal #1

I Can Eat an Elephant! - *Create bite-size goals*

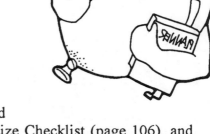

YOU'LL NEED: Copy of invitation (page 111) on colored cardstock paper, two My Bite-size Checklist (page 106), and a zip-close plastic bag for each girl, scissors, pencils, washable markers, timer, and Success Snacks.

INVITATION: Color invitation, fill in details, cut up elephant invitation, place in plastic bag, and deliver.

BITE-SIZE TIME PLANS: Tell girls, "A goal is only a dream until it is written down and achieved step-by-step." Here's How:
1. Give each girl 2 copies of the My Bite-size Checklist page (page 106), which will give girls two checklists to try and one as a master to copy.
2. Tell girls they can eat an elephant or achieve hard-to-reach goals by taking them a bite at a time. Talk about the importance of breaking long-range goals into short steps. Talk about projects at school such as a report or display, at home such as a sewing project, or getting ready for a piano recital.

HOW TO USE CHECKLISTS AND CALENDARS:
1. Challenge girls to write a long-range goal at the top of the Bite-size Checklist.
2. Write 6 bite-size steps to achieve that goal.
3. Write steps #1-6 on the calendar, projecting goal plans weeks ahead.
4. Girls can color elephant parts #1-6 bit-by-bit as they achieve. When goal is complete, color the entire elephant!

BEAT THE CLOCK: Using the Bite-size Checklist, list some projects you would like the girls to help you with, i.e. clean a room, sew on a button, clean a cupboard, mop a floor, dust, mend a sock.
Set the timer for 5 minutes for each room to clean or to work on each project. Girls can all chip in and help. When the timer rings, stop and go to the next project on the list. This will help girls get started on unwanted projects, and learn to be flexible as they have to stop for interruptions.

SUCCESS SNACKS: <u>Giant Peanut Shaped Cookies (Elephant's Favorite Snack)</u>.
Cream together: 1/2 cup margarine or butter (room temperature) 1/2 cup brown sugar, 1/2 cup granulated sugar, 1 egg, and 1 teaspoon vanilla. Combine and add: 1 3/4 cups flour, 1/4 teaspoon salt, 1 1/4 teaspoons baking soda. Shape into 1 1/2" balls, roll in granulated sugar, pinch balls in the middle. Stick a fork in rounded edges. Bake 375° 8-10 minutes.

My Bite-size Checklist

I can eat an elephant, if I take it a bite at a time, or achieve bite-size goals!

G O A L :

_____

_____

Achieve by _____ *(date)*

 #1 _____

_____

 #2 _____

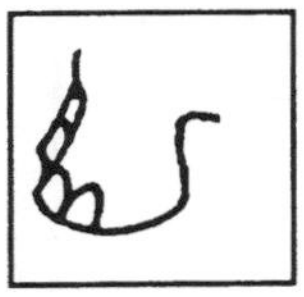

_____

 #3 _____

_____

 #4 _____

_____

 #5 _____

_____

 #6 _____

My Bite-size Checklist

I can eat an elephant, if I take it a bite at a time, or achieve bite-size goals!

G O A L :

_____

_____

Achieve by _____ *(date)*

#1 _____

_____

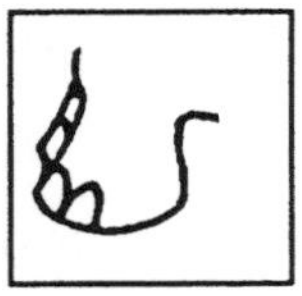

#2 _____

_____

#3 _____

_____

#4 _____

_____

 #5 _____

_____

  #6 _____

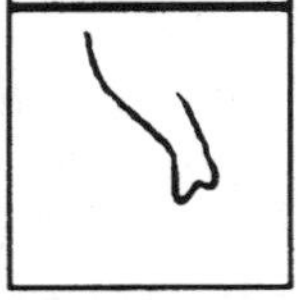

Personal Preparedness: Goal #2

My Cents-able Savings Plan - *Learn to save money*

YOU'LL NEED:
1. Copies of invitation (page 111), and 3 copies of play money coins (page 108) on colored cardstock paper for each girl.
2. Copy 1 set of the Cents-able Savings Plan #1-5 envelope labels (page 109) on lightweight paper for each girl.
3. Copy 1 or more sets of the Ooo-la-moo-la! play money (page 110) on green lightweight paper for each girl.
4. Five envelopes for each girl, scissors, washable markers, and Success Snacks.

INVITATION: Color and cut out invitation, fill in details, and deliver. Invitation asks girls to bring a wish list (things they wish to buy).

CENTS-ABLE SAVINGS PLANS:
1. Have girls project a long-range purchase for which they will need to save money, i.e. bicycle.
2. Have girls write on a piece of paper the allowance or money they are currently earning per week or month, i.e. $5 per week.
3. Ask the girls to divide and place money ($5) into Cents-able Savings Plan envelopes #1-5:
   ♥ Envelope #1 Tithing 10% (50 cents)
   ♥ Envelope #2 Gifts $20% ($1)
   ♥ Envelope #3 Mission/College 10% (50 cents)
   ♥ Envelope #4 Long-range purchase 40% ($2)
   ♥ Envelope #5 Spending 20% ($1)

4. Ask girls to cut out the play money and labels for envelopes. Glue labels on envelopes and begin dividing their money. Project this $5 into the future. Example: If you save $1 or $2 per week, what will you have in the future? Suggest girls keep play money for Super Sitter's Kit (to play store with children they tend).

OO-LA-MOO-LA! GAME: You'll need one set of play money (pages 108-110) for each girl to cut out. Tell the girls: "Oo-la" means fun and "moo-la" means money. Let's have some fun with money! TO PLAY: 1) Stand in a circle with play money in your hands. 2) Each girl takes an odd or even number to divide into teams. 3) At the count of 10, girls throw money into the air and race to gather as much cash as they can for their team.
4) The richest team earns a prize (i.e. Success Snack). Play game several times, and then divide the money evenly to take home.

SUCCESS SNACKS (Game Prizes): <u>Money Roll-ups</u>. Pretend fruit roll-ups are dollar bills. Roll them

Cents-able Money Plans
Tithing - 10%

Cents-able Money Plans
Gifts - 20%

Cents-able Money Plans
Misson/College - 10%

Cents-able Money Plans
Spending - 20%

Cents-able Money Plans
Long-range Purchase - 40%

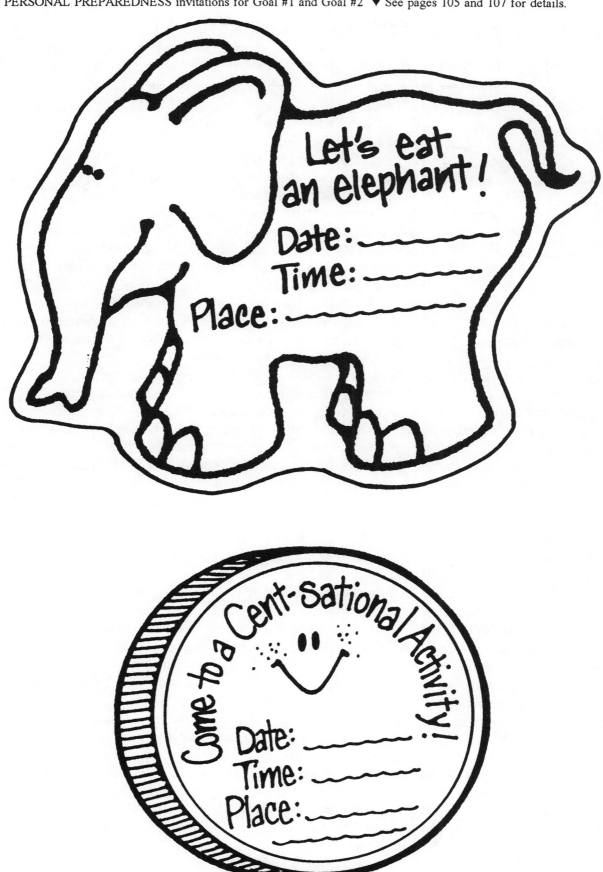

Safety & Emergency Preparedness: Goal #1

I Can Be Safe - *Learn do's and don'ts of personal safety*

YOU'LL NEED: Copies of invitation (page 119) and 72-Hour Survival Kit, and kit list/backpack pattern (pages 113-114) on colored cardstock paper for each girl, clear contact paper, scissors, washable markers, glue, pillow-slip backpack supplies (page 114), and Success Snacks.

INVITATION: Make and deliver a week ahead.

PREPAREDNESS: Talk to girls about personal safety at home and away, and during disaster situations. Encourage girls to listen to the Spirit. Live so you can be worthy of warnings from the Holy Ghost when they come. If during a fire or earthquake when your family members are separated, you must have a central meeting place and a relative or friend that everyone can call. Memorize phone number. Prepare a 72-hour kit you can take with you to school or grab and go (see Survival Supplies*).

EMERGENCY DRILL: DO have a drill so that each family member knows exactly what to expect and how to save him/herself. Disasters are frightening, and drills help prevent panic.

IN CASE OF FIRE: DON'T stand up when smoke is present, CRAWL. The smoke can be blacker than night and no visibility except on the floor; the only place you can breathe. DO know where to crawl; because of the heat you can become lost. DO keep your mind on getting out. DO establish where you are in the room and then move on out. DON'T inhale smoke. DO keep your mouth closed. DO sleep with your bedroom door closed at night in case of fire. DON'T open the door if you smell smoke. DO touch it with the back of your hand so you won't burn your palm. You will need your palms for crawling. DON'T open the door if it is hot. If you do, you add air or oxygen to the flames and they will rush in. DON'T hide in a closet. DO tie sheets together and drop from the window. DON'T open window until you are ready exit. DO have smoke alarms installed and check them monthly. DO call 911 if you hear the smoke alarm go off or smell smoke. DO use a fire extinguisher: pull pin out, point nozzle to base of fire, and spray. DON'T run if you are on fire, but STOP, DROP, and ROLL.

IN CASE OF EARTHQUAKE: DO take a CERT (Community Emergency Response Team) training course with your parents. Call the fire department to become a part of their help team. DO keep a pair of shoes under your bed you can slip on, and a flashlight so you can find your way in the dark. DO have your parents show you how to shut off the water and gas in your home, where the fire extinguishers are, and how to use them. When the earth is shaking, crawl under a table or desk or door frame even after the quake is over. An aftershock minutes later can be worse.

HOME SAFETY: DO follow cooking safety rules. DO keep all doors locked and check them before parents leave. DON'T open the door when parents are not home.

SAFETY AWAY FROM HOME: DO use caution if someone in a car slows down beside you when you are walking alone. If someone stops a car to ask you questions, use caution. Stand back, don't get close to the car, and prepare to run if you sense danger. DON'T take a ride home with someone until you check with your parents first. DO walk home from school with someone, and use the same caution as you would if you were alone.

*SURVIVAL SUPPLIES: Make 72-Hour Kit pillow-slip backpack (pages 113-114) so girls can start collecting survival supplies and have a place to store them.

SUCCESS SNACKS: <u>Survival Snacks</u>. Share an emergency meal or dried fruit.

PATTERN: 72-Hour Kit survival list and instructions on how to make a pillow-slip backpack

72-Hour Kit Survival List
- ♥ Battery power radio
- ♥ Flashlight/batteries
- ♥ First-aid kit ♥ Comb
- ♥ Matches (waterproofed)
- ♥ Compass ♥ Soap
- ♥ Adhesive tape 1" wide in 12" strips
- ♥ Small pocketknife
- ♥ Bendable wire 5'-10'
- ♥ Fishing lures, flies, sinkers, and hooks
- ♥ Heavy nylon fishline
- ♥ Water purifying tablets
- ♥ Heavy aluminum foil
- ♥ Collapsable cup
- ♥ Pencil and paper
- ♥ Whistle and flares
- ♥ Jacket ♥ Extra socks
- ♥ Blanket ♥ Plastic bags
- ♥ Dehydrated food, canned meats & juice, peanut butter, crackers, K-rations, candy, gum, 6-8 meal packets, 6-8 energy bars, 5-6 bullion cubes, powdered milk
- ♥ Water (2 1/2 gallons)
- ♥ Toilet paper
- ♥ Lip gloss
- ♥ Can opener
- ♥ Sunscreen
- ♥ Lotion
- ♥ Safety pins
- ♥ Emergency manual
- ♥ First-aid manual
- ♥ Feminine supplies

72-Hour Kit Survival List
- ♥ Battery power radio
- ♥ Flashlight/batteries
- ♥ First-aid kit ♥ Comb
- ♥ Matches (waterproofed)
- ♥ Compass ♥ Soap
- ♥ Adhesive tape 1" wide in 12" strips
- ♥ Small pocketknife
- ♥ Bendable wire 5'-10'
- ♥ Fishing lures, flies, sinkers, and hooks
- ♥ Heavy nylon fishline
- ♥ Water purifying tablets
- ♥ Heavy aluminum foil
- ♥ Collapsable cup
- ♥ Pencil and paper
- ♥ Whistle and flares
- ♥ Jacket ♥ Extra socks
- ♥ Blanket ♥ Plastic bags
- ♥ Dehydrated food, canned meats & juice, peanut butter, crackers, K-rations, candy, gum, 6-8 meal packets, 6-8 energy bars, 5-6 bullion cubes, powdered milk
- ♥ Water (2 1/2 gallons)
- ♥ Toilet paper
- ♥ Lip gloss
- ♥ Can opener
- ♥ Sunscreen
- ♥ Lotion
- ♥ Safety pins
- ♥ Emergency manual
- ♥ First-aid manual
- ♥ Feminine supplies

How to Make a 72-Hour Backpack:
You'll Need: A pillow slip, 90" of fabric rope or cord, scissors, needle and thread, pencil, fabric paint or laundry pen, and 72-Hour Kit pattern (page 113) to trace.

MAKE BAG:
1. Cut two 1" slits on both sides of seam in pillow hem.
2. Thread 50" of fabric rope or cord through slit #1 and back out slit #2.
3. Tie knots on fabric rope or cord on both ends so rope won't slip back through.
4. Attach two pieces of 20" fabric rope or cord on top left and right side.
5. Attach in middle on left and right side to allow girls to slip arms through backpack.
6. Be sure to sew through both layers of fabric for reinforcement.

DECORATE BAG:
1. Tape the 72-Hour Kit pattern (page 113) up to the window.
2. Tape the pillow slip up to window.
3. Trace 72-Hour Kit pattern with a pencil.
4. Go over pencil tracings with a laundry marker or decorate with fabric paints.

FILL BAG:
1. If bag is too long, pull part of back up and sew in pockets.
2. Fill bag with 72-hour survival items found on list. Keep one list next to your shopping list and the other in the backpack.

Safety & Emergency Preparedness: Goal #2

First Aid Station - *Learn Florence Nightingale's Secrets*

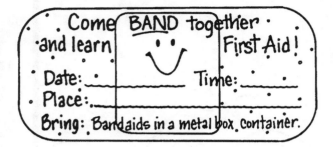

Come **BAND** together
and learn   First Aid!
Date: _____ Time: _____
Place: _____
Bring: Bandaids in a metal box container.

YOU'LL NEED: Copies of invitation (page 119), Band-aid Box First Aid Kit label, first aid flip chart (pages 117-118) on colored cardstock paper, and two 3/4" binder rings for each girl, clear contact paper, scissors, washable markers, glue, paper punch, band-aid boxes, first aid kit samples*, and Snacks.

INVITATION: Make and deliver a week ahead.

FLORENCE NIGHTINGALE'S SECRETS: Ask a girl to review the book *Florence Nightingale* by Anne Colver from the book series *A Discovery Biography* (Chelsea House, 1992). Florence was a war nurse who lived in England in the 1800s. She was asked by the head of the war department to nurse the wounded soldiers in the war between England and Russia. She took 40 nurses with her, taking supplies and nurse uniforms. There were stories in the newspaper about Florence every day. Her family was proud of her. *"The prayers of all England were with them."* They found the soldiers with bloody bandages on their arms and legs, too sick to move, lying on the icy ground. The nurses were very tired and sick when they got there, but they forgot about themselves and went to work.

Head Injury: DO NOT move victim unless in immediate danger. Keep head and neck from moving by placing hands on both sides of the head. Send someone to call 911. Keep victim warm, not hot.

SECRETS: WHAT DID FLORENCE AND HER NURSES DO? At any time you may be required to set up a first aid station as Florence did. You will need to know these First Aid Trade Secrets A-Z: **B**ites, Animal and Human, **B**ites, Snake, **B**leeding and Open Wounds, **B**urns, **C**hoking, un**C**onscious, **C**olds & Cough, Communicable Disease, Convulsions & Seizures, **D**iabetic Emergencies, **E**ars, **E**yes, **F**ainting, **F**alls, **G**astrointestinal, **H**eadache, **H**ead Injuries, **N**ose Injuries, **P**ediculosis (bugs or head lice), **P**oisoning, **S**kin Infections, Splinters, Sprains, Fractures and Dislocations, Stings & Insect Bites, **T**eeth (some health-ful hints are on pages 117-118).

FIRST AID STATION: Color and cut out cards (pages 117-118), laminate and punch holes on the left. Place two 3/4" binder rings in holes to keep cards together. After completing cards, demonstrate each technique with supplies on hand. Ask a person to demonstrate the Heimlich Maneuver (see choking), CPR, and rescue breathing (call the American Red Cross). For emergency help in some cities call the ASK-A-NURSE, doctor, or 911.

*FIRST AID KITS:

#1 Band-aid Box Kit: Color and cut out labels (page 116), laminate, and tape onto a band-aid box. Fill box with small kit supplies listed on page 116.

#2 Gallon Ice Cream Carton Kit: Add supplies listed on page 116.

SUCCESS SNACKS:

American Red Cross Cookies: Make sugar cookie recipe (page 80), reserving 3/4 cup dough (color with red food coloring). Roll out cookies and cut into round shapes. Roll out red dough and cut into long 1/2" x 2" strips to make a red cross. Place cross on top of cookies and bake at 350° 8-10 minutes.

The American Red Cross has millions of volunteers in hospitals and community agencies giving money, blood, training, and first aid to disaster victims in emergency, and emergency prevention. National headquarters: 1-(703)-206-6000, or check for local help.

First Aid Kit

First Aid Safety Rules:
Call 911 if Child is:

♥ Choking ♥ Not breathing ♥ Bleeding won't stop ♥ Broken bones or dislocated ♥ Burned ♥ Poisoned ♥ Snake bite ♥ Animal bite or insect sting

Learn and Follow First Aid Rules

HOW TO USE BAND-AID BOX

FIRST AID KIT:

1. Stop bleeding.
2. Wash dirt out of wound.
3. Use tweezers to pull out slivers.
4. Place antiseptic cream on wound.
5. Place bandage on wound.
6. ♥ Kiss it better (x o x o x).

SMALL KIT should contain: Alcohol wipes, antibacterial ointment, bandages, gauze pads, safety pins, thermometer, and tweezers

LARGE KIT (gallon ice cream carton): Add items from small kit list above plus the following: Absorbent cotton, ace bandage, adhesive bandage tape, alcohol (70%) or alcohol based wipes, bandages (1" and 2"), cotton tipped applicators, disposable tissue, ice bag, latex gloves, quick reference first aid manual, medical bandages (assorted sizes), tongue depressors, triangle bandage for sling (30" or 40") scissors, soap, sterile gauze pads (3" x 3", 2" x 2"), and syrup of Ipecac to induce vomiting (only if Poison Control advises).

TOP PRIORITY CHILD CARE:
Safety First - Anticipate the Worst

♥ Keep small items away from a child under 3 ♥ Be as careful as you can be
♥ Keep doors locked and children safe

Place pattern on can lid.
Pattern fits 3" x 4" bandage box or can.

Insect Stings:

If you know person has severe reaction to insect bites, seek medical help immediately (if you suspect sting may be poisonous). If  person has medicine for their allergic reactions, help them take it. For minor stings, remove visible stinger by scraping skin, wash, and apply cold compress or mud (mix dirt with water or use facial mud mask).

Broken Bones:

DO NOT move person unless in danger. DO NOT move injured parts. Control bleeding. Cover bone that sticks out with a clean moist cloth. Call 911. Don't give food or drink; they may be in shock. Keep them warm. If you have to move person, keep injured area from  moving by placing a piece of wood or folded towel or tie a blanket over and under injury.

Convulsion/ Seizure:

Person has jerking movements, bluish face and lips, eyes rolled back, clenched teeth, and frothing mouth (convulsions end in less than 30 seconds). After, they can enter into a  drowsy or unconscious state. Keep person from hurting themselves during convulsion. Don't hold them or put object between their teeth. After, don't give food or drink. Lay on side and check breathing. Call 911 or seek medical aid.

Drowning:

Try to rescue first by handing them a pole or rope. Don't try to swim to victim unless you are trained to rescue. If person is not breathing, have someone begin CPR. If no  pulse but person is breathing, begin rescue breathing. Send someone to call 911.

Electric Shock:

Send someone to call 911. Don't touch victim until power has been disconnected. Unplug or switch off electrical source. If not breathing or has no pulse, have someone begin CPR. If victim has pulse but is 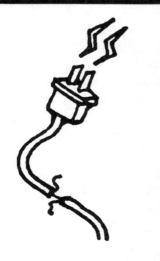 not breathing, begin rescue breathing.

Head Injury:

DO NOT move victim unless in immediate danger. Keep head and neck from moving by placing hands on both sides of the head. Send someone to call 911. Keep victim warm, not hot.

Dog/Animal Bites:

Wash wound with running water. Control bleeding. Bandage with clean dry dressing. Seek medical help. Find help to capture animal to test for rabies.

Bleeding and Wounds:

Place gauze or clean cloth, or gloved hand over wound and apply firm steady pressure. Don't remove bandage. Call 911 to seek help. Elevate injured leg or arm above heart.

Burns:

Place burned area in cool water or place gently apply a cool compress for 5 minutes. Do not use ointments. Clip leaf from Aloe Vera plant, squirt out juice, and apply to burn. Bandage. Call 911 if burn is blistered.

Choking:

Let person speak or cough to see if they have air or cough out object. Call 911 if they can't get air. Abdominal Thrusts: Stand behind, wrap arms around waist. Make fist with hand, place above navel and below ribs. With thumb and fingers press toward you. Grab fist with other hand and pull it toward you quickly pushing upward. Repeat until person breathes.

Poison:

If there is pain in throat or stomach, drowsiness, vomiting, or unconsciousness, call Poison Control Center or 911 and follow their exact directions. Keep poison or any vomit. Don't give anything by mouth unless told to.

Eye Injury:

Chemical: Hold eyelids apart and flush eyeball with lukewarm running water until ambulance arrives. Place gauze pad/bandage over eye.
Imbedded Object, Cut or Scratch: Don't try to remove imbedded object. Place gauze over eye and secure with bandage. Get to emergency room.

PATTERN: SAFETY & EMERGENCY PREP. invitations for Goal #1 and Goal #2 ♥ See pages 112 and 115 for details.

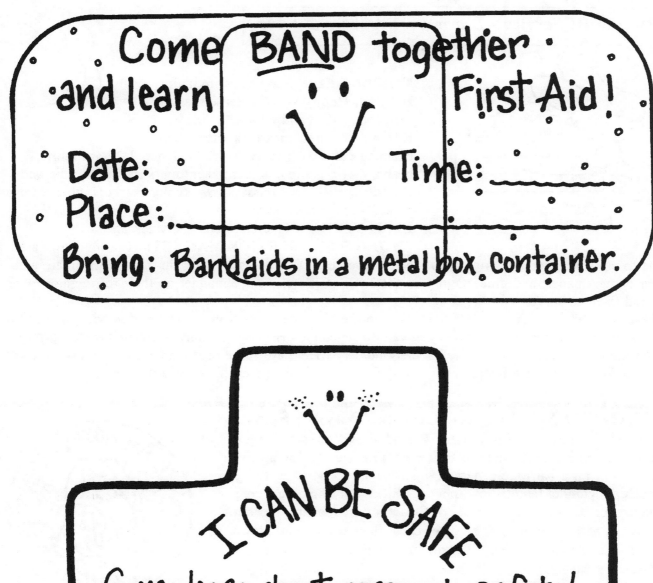

Come BAND together and learn First Aid!

Date: _____ Time: _____

Place: _____

Bring: Bandaids in a metal box container.

I CAN BE SAFE

Come learn about personal safety!

Date: Time:

Place:

Service & Citizenship: Goal #1

| Hop to It! Service - *Learn creative ways to serve* |

YOU'LL NEED: Copies of invitation and I am Hoppy When I Serve magnet card (page 124) and Hop to it! ideas below on colored cardstock paper, bunny beanbag pattern (page 121), 1/2" magnet, 1/2 yard fabric, beans, fabric pompoms, permanent markers, and needle and thread for each girl, scissors, watercolor markers, glue, contact paper, and Success Snacks.

INVITATION: Make and deliver a week ahead.

"HOP TO IT!" SERVICE MAGNET: The invitation asks girls to color magnet and bring it to the Achievement Days activity. Cut out magnet, laminate with clear contact paper, and glue magnet on the back. Girls can place magnet on their refrigerator to remind them to serve.

"HOP TO IT!" SERVICE IDEAS: Talk to the girls about ways they can be of service, and follow up on one or two service activities you can do together, i.e. make a bunny beanbag for the nursery and volunteer to help in the Relief Society nursery. Here are some more ideas the girls can do (copy this list for girls to take home or glue in their Service and Citizenship journal divider page):

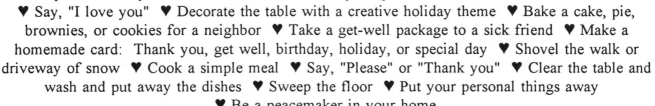

HOP TO IT! Fun and Creative Ways to Serve

♥ Plant or weed a flower garden ♥ Find an old folks' home and adopt a grandma or grandpa to treat with TLC (tender loving care) Ideas: Put on a patriotic program, a Christmas concert, Halloween costume parade, talent show, play or skit, family home evening, reading of books, or long talks ♥ Clean out a cupboard, closet or drawer ♥ Help brother or sister clean their room, then play a game or read together ♥ Learn fun jokes or stories to tell ♥ Wear a cheerful smile ♥ Greet the day with a song ♥ Make a candy bar poster to relay a message of friendship or get-well wishes ♥ Tend children free in your home so parents can attend the temple ♥ Pack your own school lunch or a surprise picnic ♥ Say, "I love you" ♥ Decorate the table with a creative holiday theme ♥ Bake a cake, pie, brownies, or cookies for a neighbor ♥ Take a get-well package to a sick friend ♥ Make a homemade card: Thank you, get well, birthday, holiday, or special day ♥ Shovel the walk or driveway of snow ♥ Cook a simple meal ♥ Say, "Please" or "Thank you" ♥ Clear the table and wash and put away the dishes ♥ Sweep the floor ♥ Put your personal things away ♥ Be a peacemaker in your home

"HOP TO IT!" BUNNY: Make beanbag bunny and donate to the nursery. Pattern is on page 121.

SUCCESS SNACKS: Hop To It! Bunnies in the Grass. Create a bunny scene on a field of green gelatin grass with pear bunnies on top. How To: Make a double batch of green gelatin and refrigerate to set (in a rectangular shaped pan). Place pear halves on top (bunny bodies), whipped cream or marshmallow (tail), almond slices (ears), and cloves or jelly bean (eyes). Cut into green gelatin dessert and serve each girl a bunny in the grass saying, "Hop to it and serve hop-pily!"

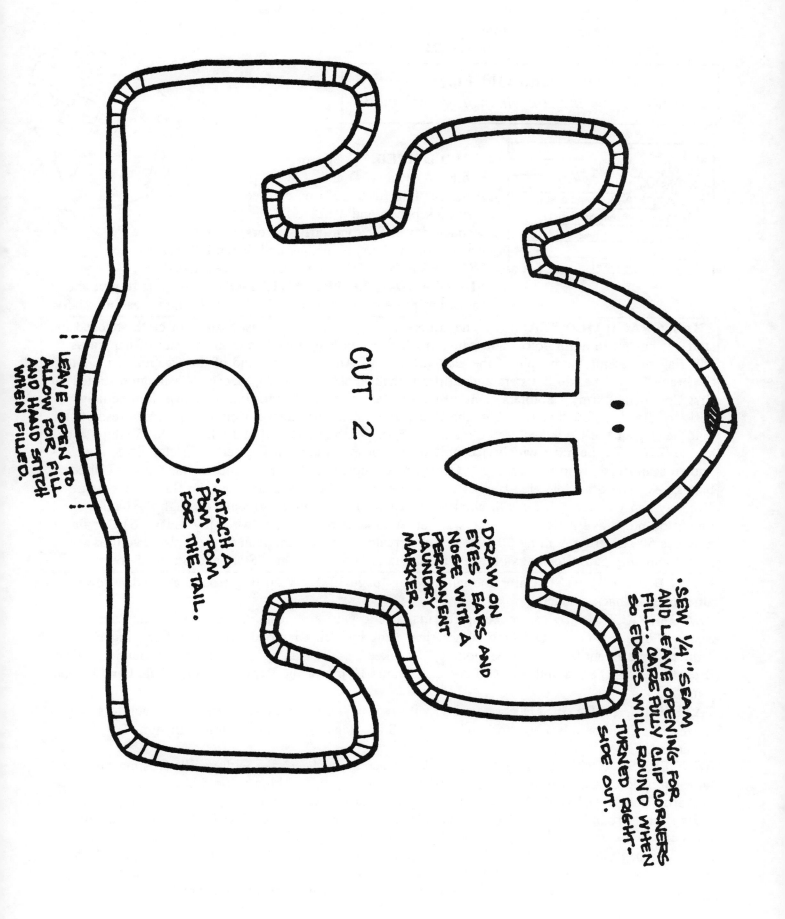

CUT 2

LEAVE OPEN TO ALLOW FOR FILL AND HAND STITCH WHEN FILLED.

· ATTACH A POM POM FOR THE TAIL.

· DRAW ON EYES, EARS AND NOSE WITH A PERMANENT LAUNDRY MARKER.

· SEW 1/4" SEAM AND LEAVE OPENING FOR FILL. CAREFULLY CLIP CORNERS SO EDGES WILL ROUND WHEN TURNED RIGHT-SIDE OUT.

Service & Citizenship: Goal #2

That Grand Old Flag:
Learn to wave the American flag with pride

YOU'LL NEED: Copies of invitation (page 124) and "I ♥ America" flag (page 123) on colored cardstock paper, and a 12" x 1/4" wooden dowel for each girl, scissors, watercolor markers, glue/tape, and Success Snacks.
INVITATION: Make and deliver a week ahead.
SHOW-AND-TELL PRESENTATION: Ask girls to give the following presentation showing the flag (take turns reading #1-5).

THAT GRAND OLD FLAG! 1) The American flag is more than just a piece of cloth attached to a staff. It has meaningful colors and patterns which mean life, liberty, and the pursuit of happiness. Our flag represents the people of the United States of America, "the land of the free and the home of the brave." 2) What do the stars and stripes mean? On July 3, 1775, George Washington started the first Continental army. Soldiers came in with different uniforms carrying their own individually-designed flags. After the signing of the Declaration of Independence, Congress passed a resolution that the flag of the United States be made of 15 stripes, alternate red and white with 15 white stars in a blue field. 3) The most widely accepted legend of the American flag tells of Betsy Ross, a well known seamstress, who was asked by George Washington to design a national flag for the United States. 4) "The Star-Spangled Banner" was a national anthem written about the flag. Let's sing: "Oh, say can you see ..." Let's think about that flag that continued to wave through the battles fought by our brave American soldiers ... battles to keep the freedom we enjoy today. 5) Our flag now has 50 stars representing 50 states. Let's create our own American flag. Let's wave it as we march and sing patriotic songs like "You're a Grand Old Flag", and "Stars and Stripes Forever."

FLAG DECORATION: Color and cut out flag (page 123). Wrap flag around a wooden dowel and glue together back to back.
FLAG MARCH: Girls can make up fun marches to patriotic music as they wave their flags. Songs: "You're a Grand Old Flag," "America" sung by Neil Diamond (from The Jazz Singer), "America the Beautiful," "Yankee Doodle," "Yankee Doodle Dandy," "Star Spangled Banner," "God Bless America," "Stars and Stripes Forever," "Battle Hymn of the Republic," and "This Land is Your Land."
PATRIOTIC PARADE: Decorate a box with red, white, and blue streamers and attach to a wagon to ride in a June or July neighborhood parade. Stick flags (page 123) on top with sign "I ♥ America."
SUCCESS SNACKS: <u>Grand Old Flag Cake</u>. Decorate a sheet cake with vanilla frosting mixed with whipped cream. Sprinkle red colored sugar for stripes, and blue colored sugar for stars. Place gumdrop stars over blue. To make gumdrop stars: Smash small white or yellow gumdrops with rolling pin to round shape. Then cut round shape into star shape. OPTION: Purchase miniature flags and place on cupcakes sprinkled with red and blue sugar. To make sugar, place granulated sugar in a bag; add drops of color and mix. Tell girls that flag code states that the flag should never be used as wearing apparel, bedding or drapery ... never be used as a costume, never touch the ground, or left out in bad weather. The flag should be flown on all national holidays.

TAB - GLUE A HERE.

A

I AM HOPPY WHEN I SERVE!

Hop on over for a fun Activity!

To: _____
Date: _____ Time: _____
Place: _____

• Glue a cottonball on the "x" for a puffy soft tail!

• Be sure to color magnet attached and bring it to the activity!

That Grand Old Flag!

You're invited over to learn about our American Flag!

Date: _____ Time: _____

Place: _____

See you there!

124

Spirituality: Goal #1

B. E. A. R. S.
Be Enthusiastic About Reading Scriptures

YOU'LL NEED: Copies of invitation (page 132), B.E.A.R.S. bookmark (page 126), and B.E.A.R.S. game board (page 127) on colored cardstock paper for each girl, scissors, watercolor markers, clear contact paper (for laminating), 6" ribbons (tie on bookmarks), and Snacks.
INVITATION: Make and deliver a week ahead.
B. E. A. R. S. ACTIVITIES: Help girls know that B.E.A.R.S. means "Be Enthusiastic About Reading Scriptures" with the following activities:
ACTIVITY #1 Create a B.E.A.R.S. bookmarks to remind girls to Be Enthusiastic About Reading Scriptures. Read John 22:29 and 2 Nephi 4:15 and other scriptures that motivate scripture reading. Tell girls that the word "enthus" is a Greek word that means "God within." When they read the scriptures, they invite the Holy Ghost to guide them. Read Moroni 10:4-5 to memorize the Book of Mormon promise.
ACTIVITY #2 Help girls find and underline scriptures that will help them Be Enthusiastic About Reading Scriptures. Ask girls to choose a subject they would like to learn about, then all girls can look up the subject and find scriptures. For example, a scripture on friendship or love is 1 John 4:7.
ACTIVITY #3 Play the B.E.A.R.S. Scripture Chase Game. Create a spinner board from the pattern on page 127. To play, divide girls into two teams with the standard works in their hand. Spin the bear. When bear paw points towards a standard work, i.e. the Book of Mormon or Pearl of Great Price, leader names a subject, i.e. faith, charity, and girls rush to find a scripture found in that standard work, using the Topical Guide. The first to find the scripture reads it and earns a point for her team. Play 15-20 minutes.
ACTIVITY #4 Sing songs that relate to the scriptures from the four standard works found in the Children's Songbook* with matching scriptures:
Example #1 *I'm Trying to Be like Jesus* on page 78. Read John 13:15, 34
Example #2 *I Love to See the Temple* on page 95. Read Doctrine and Covenants 124:39-41
Example #3 *Search, Ponder, and Pray* on page 109. Read 2 Nephi 4:15, and Mosiah 1:6-7
Example #4 *I Will Be Valiant* on page 162. Read Alma 53:20-21
Example #5 *Saturday* on page 196. Read Exodus 20:10-11
HAVE A TESTIMONY MEETING: Share your testimony of the scriptures and allow girls to "bear" their testimony about the scriptures to show their enthusiasm for the scriptures.
SUCCESS SNACKS: Treat #1 Bear Marshmallow/Rice Treats. Follow the recipe on the *Kellogg's* Rice Krispies cereal box and mold treat into bear-shaped molds. Spray molds with cooking spray first. Place heart-shaped cinnamon candy nose and chocolate chip eyes in mold, then press treat into mold. Treat #2 Cinnamon Bear Cupcakes. Make cupcakes, frost and top with four cinnamon bears representing the four standard works. Talk to girls about the four standard works and why they should Be Enthusiastic About Reading Scriptures.
Children's Songbook is published by The Church of Jesus Christ of Latter-day Saints, Salt Lake City, Utah.

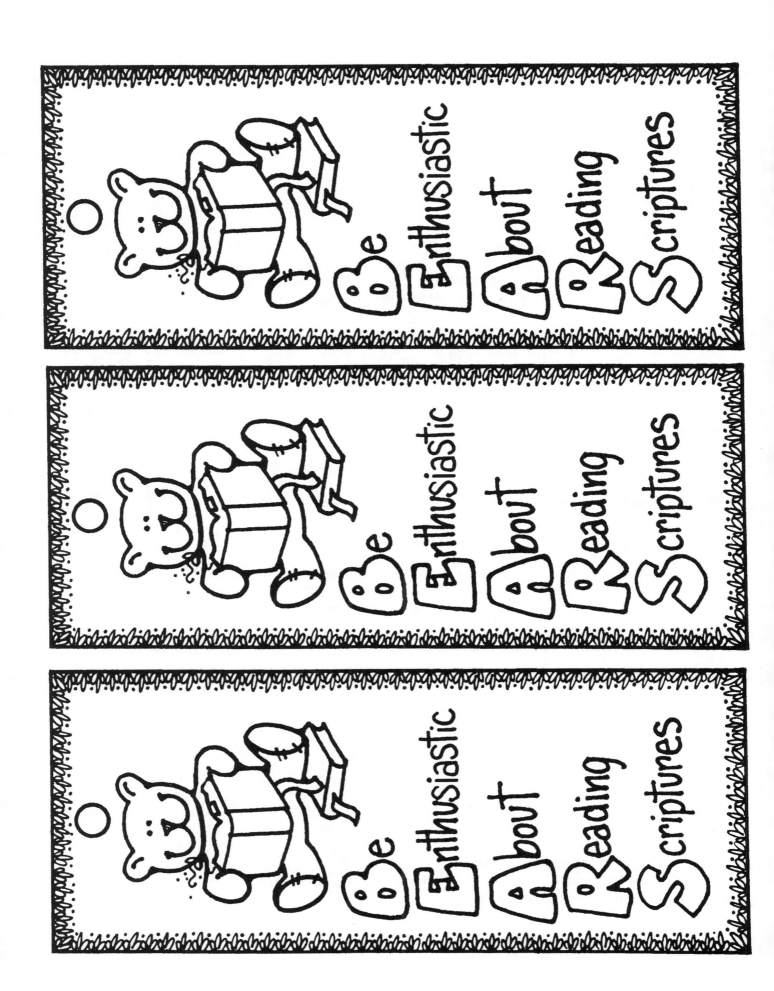

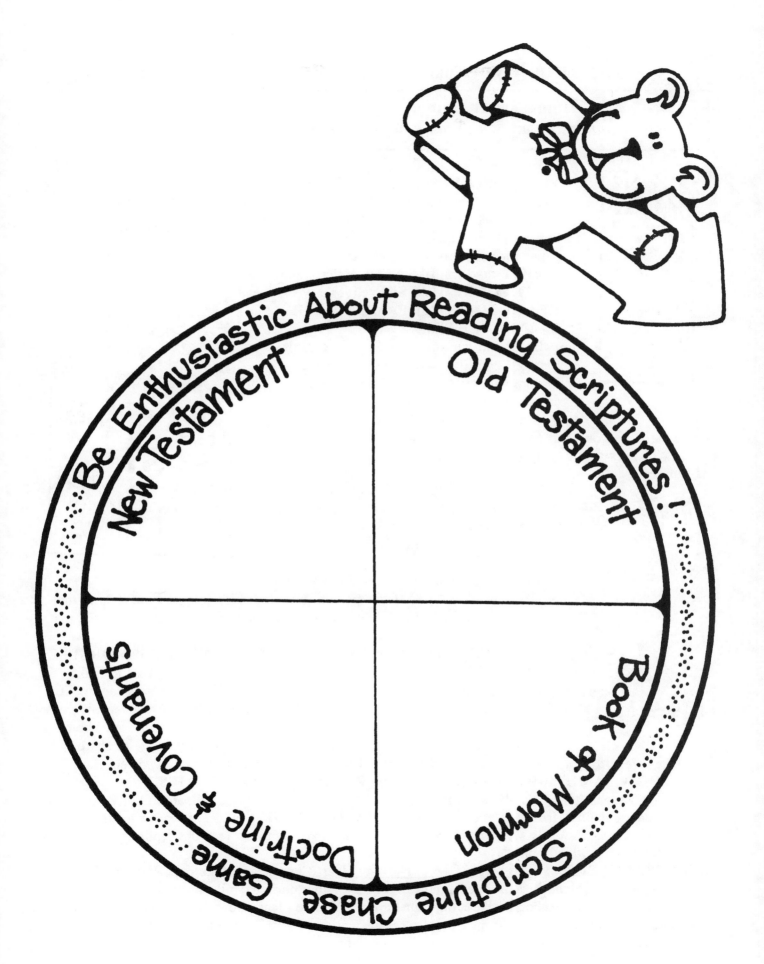

Be Enthusiastic About Reading Scriptures!

New Testament

Old Testament

Book of Mormon

Doctrine & Covenants

Scripture Chase Game

Spirituality: Goal #2

Home Sweet Home:
Sweeten your testimony with family home evening

YOU'LL NEED: Copies of invitation (page 132) and Heart-to-Heart Family Home Evening Chart and name cards (pages 129-130), and Families are Special puzzle (page 131) on colored cardstock paper for each girl, clear contact paper, scissors, washable markers, sticky-back Velcro, and Success Snacks.

INVITATION: Make and deliver a week ahead.

HEART-TO-HEART FAMILY HOME EVENING CHART:

1. Color and cut out chart and name cards (pages 129-130). Write names on cards.

2. Laminate chart and cards with clear contact paper.

3. Attach sticky-back Velcro on back of name cards and on chart to attach cards to chart.

4. Talk to girls about using chart, placing name cards next to the assignments.

FAMILIES ARE SPECIAL PUZZLE: Encourage girls to do the following: Color and cut out the missing family puzzle (page 131). Put puzzle together with your family and talk about what it would be like if one person in your family was missing (taking that one person out of the puzzle). Tell what you would miss about that person.

HOW TO MAKE FAMILY HOME EVENINGS MEMORABLE:

1. Use your Heart-to-Heart Family Home Evening Chart to make assignments, i.e. music, prayer, scripture, lesson, activity, and treat.

2. Practice a family home evening presentation at Achievement Days. Divide girls into two teams. Each team can present a family home evening to the other team. Then girls can take it home to share.

3. Make a record in a Family Home Evening Journal of activities your family enjoyed repeating.

HOW FAMILY HOME EVENING SUPER SCRIPTURE ACTIVITIES:

We suggest that girls choose from the already-developed, theme-coordinated family home evenings from the books *SUPER SCRIPTURE ACTIVITIES: I'm Trying to Be Like Jesus, Jesus Is My Friend, and Tell Me the Stories of Jesus* (see descriptions in the back of this book).

SUCCESS SNACKS: Home Sweet Home, Heart-to-Heart Cupcakes. Make cupcakes for girls topped with frosting and heart-shaped candies. Tell girls that during family home evening you can have some great heart-to-heart talks with your family. You can learn how they really feel about you and about themselves, and about the gospel of Jesus Christ. Use this time to get to know your family. Sweeten your testimony with family home evening.

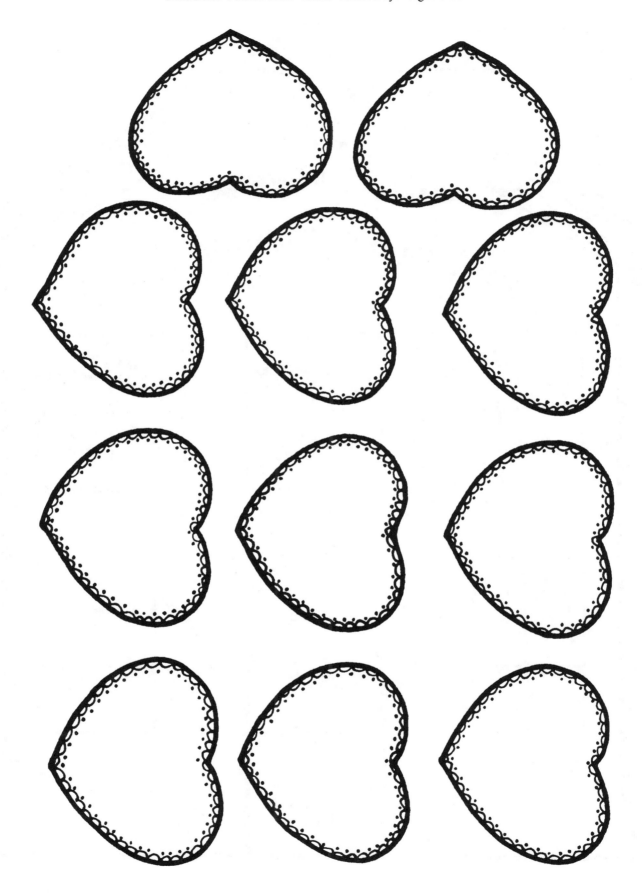

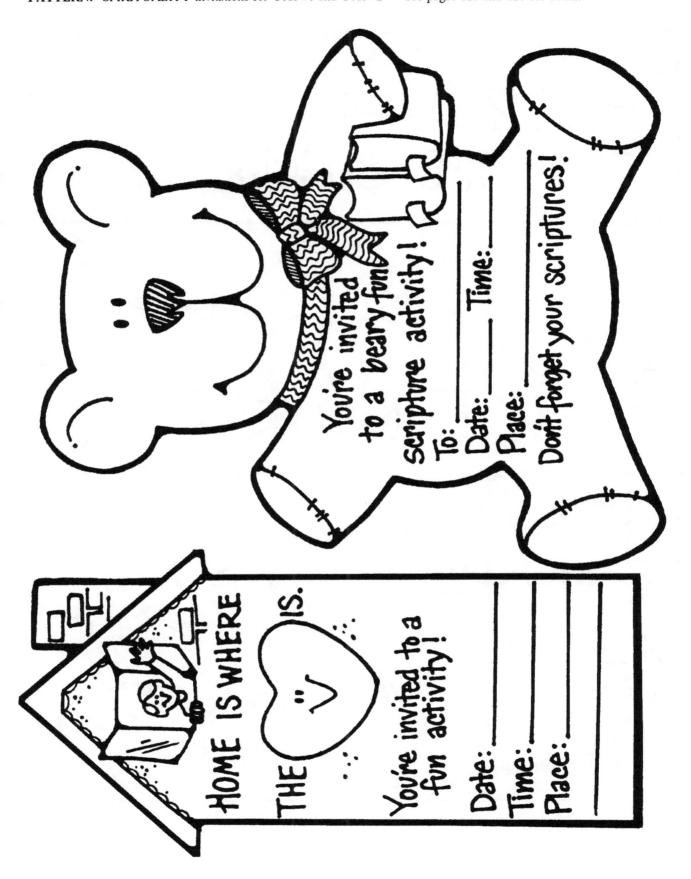

You're invited to a beary fun scripture activity!

To:

Date: _____ Time: _____

Place: _____

Don't forget your scriptures!

HOME IS WHERE THE ♥ IS.

You're invited to a fun activity!

Date: _____

Time: _____

Place: _____

Sports & Physical Fitness: Goal #1

Three Cheers for Good Sports!
Learn to play three sports cheerfully

YOU'LL NEED: Copies of invitation (page 138) and sportsmanship medal (page 134) on colored cardstock paper, and 12" wide ribbon to attach to medal for each girl, scissors, washable markers, glue, sports equipment, and Success Snacks.

INVITATION: Make and deliver a week ahead.

THREE CHEERS FOR GOOD SPORTS!
Talk to girls about the three rules of good sportsmanship before introducing three different sports (ideas below).
Tell girls that sports is as easy as 1, 2, 3. Here's how:
1) Learn how to play, 2) Give it a try, and 3) Be a good sport.

Here Are Three ways to be a GOOD SPORT:

Cheer #1 <u>Good Sport Cheer #1 Follow the golden rule</u>: Do unto others as you would have them do unto you. If you like to hear "Good play," say it.

Cheer #2 <u>Good Sport Cheer #2 Smile</u>. A cheerful face is a fun-tastic way to make friends. Smile, especially when you goof at sports.

Cheer #3 <u>Good Sport Cheer #3 Be courteous</u>. When it's another person's turn to play, give them a chance to show what they can do.

HERE ARE THREE SPORTS TO CHEER ABOUT ... It's a Triple-Header*:

SPORT #1 Laundry Basketball: This indoor sport is a terrific way to shoot for baskets with balls or balloons into a laundry basket. Divide into teams and take turns shooting for points. If playing on stairs, give higher stairs more points. Start with 10 points for the lower stair and 50 for the higher. Girls can also play catch using the laundry basket for a mitt.

SPORT #2 Frisbee Baseball: Chart out a baseball diamond with three bases and home plate. Divide into teams with team #1 in the field and team #2 up at home plate. Person who is up throws the Frisbee out into the field. Players try to catch Frisbee. If they do, it's an automatic out! Player runs the bases 1, 2, and 3 and then home. If outfield players touch before they reach the base, they are out! After 3 outs players switch places. Play for 30 minutes. Winning teams scores the most runs. Home runs count double!

SPORT #3 Water Balloon Volleyball: It's a blast! What we mean is, players go to the hose, place balloons over hose with small stream of water, fill up balloons, tie them and you have 5 or 10 balloons to burst over a net. Play with regular volleyball rules, rotating positions and serving, only throw the ball-oon instead of hitting it. Players on the other side are to catch the ball-oon without it bursting. When it bursts they lose a point to the other team, no matter who serves. The team with the most popped balloons loses ... cheerfully but wet!

SPORTS AWARDS: Color, cut, out, and place two ribbons at the bottom of the sportsmanship medal (page 134) for each girl and present in Primary.

CREATIVE PLAY: Encourage girls to be creative and make up their own versions of different sports. The more creative they are, the more memories created and friendships made. Talk to them about creativity and what it is. It is doing something usual in an unusual way.

SUCCESS SNACKS: *<u>Triple-Header Cones</u>. Give girls a three scoops ice cream and say together, "Ice-cream" when we win at sports! A *triple-header program consists of three consecutive games. Learn fun sports motto: "It's better to be a good sport than to be good at sports."

You're a berry good sport!

You're a berry good sport!

You're a berry good sport!

You're a berry good sport!

Sports & Physical Fitness: Goal #2

Freta Frog's Fitness Fun:
Enjoy "ribbit" ... heart pumping exercises

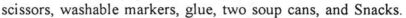

YOU'LL NEED: Copies of invitation (page 138) and Freta Frog's Fitness Fun exercise poster (pages 136-137) on colored cardstock paper for each girl, scissors, washable markers, glue, two soup cans, and Snacks.
INVITATION: Make and deliver a week ahead.
FRETA FROG'S FITNESS FUN: Allow girls to color and cut out poster (pages 136-137), gluing parts A and B together. Talk about poster and say, "Let's talk about Freta Frog's heart pumping exercises. Ribbit ... ribbit! Freta Frog is at it again! Day after day her heart beats faster and faster as she does her heart pumping exercises ... pumping blood to the body cells. This increases her energy as it makes her body strong. She ribbits up her motor and away she goes! After she exercises, Freta reads her pulse. She waits 15 seconds and finds her pulse (wrist or neck). She counts the beats for 15 seconds, then multiplies that number by four. This will give her the number of beats per minute. Example: 26 beats in 15 seconds is 26 x 4 = 104. She knows that a hard workout is 140 to 160 beats per minute. Freta jumps a little longer and a little harder the next time to increase her ribbit-ability. She started her fitness program with 2 minutes a day, then 5, then ribbits up to 15-20 minutes of heart pumping exercises... ribbit!" She knows exercise is fun. **Freta's motto is: Don't be a toad, sitting on your lily pad all day ... get up and move ... exercise is play!"**
WHY DO WE NEED EXERCISE? With over 600 muscles in your body, they need movement to stay healthy. If you break a bone, the doctor would put a cast on it to keep the bones from moving, allowing it to heal. After six weeks the muscles will be lame, weak, and hard to move. The doctor will ask you to strengthen your muscles with exercise to keep your body from getting lame. If your muscles are firm (flex arm to see), then you will look healthy and feel healthy. As you exercise, your heart and bones get stronger. Daily exercise and eating lots of calcium-rich foods will help prevent osteoporosis, a crippling bone disease.
ENJOY EXERCISE: Exercise by yourself, with your family, or with a friend. Start out slowly and work up to 20 minutes three times a week to get your heart pumping. Warm up by stretching muscles before you exercise. Cool down after vigorous activity with five minutes of slow walking, swimming, or other mild exercise. Move until the pulse rate slows down to less than one 100 beats per minute.
KINDS OF EXERCISE: Start with the Freta Frog's Fitness Fun plan for a total body exercise. Then enjoy fast walking, running/jogging, turning somersaults, lap swimming, bike riding, rope jumping, climbing stairs, weeding, housework, dancing and aerobic dancing, gymnastics, ice skating or roller-skating, and sports like batting and catching a ball, bowling, tennis, table tennis, Frisbee, basketball, or soccer. You can exercise by lifting weights. Start stretching out with a soup can in each hand. Demonstrate simple weight lifting, i.e. lifting up and out, down halfway to chest, and in.
SUCCESS SNACKS: <u>Fruit Juice or Fresh Fruit</u>. Tell girls, "Fruit is a natural sugar, a treat that will give you energy or pep. Try drinking 6-8 glasses of water each day. Water washes away toxins or poisons and replaces lost moisture. An apple a day helps, as it's 85% water."

Party #3 THEME: Dad and Me: Western Jamboree
OBJECTIVE: Sheriff dad and deputy daughter catch the spirit of the Old West as they enjoy un-citified games, western dancin' lessons, and cowboy/cowgirl grub. Ya-hoo!
YOU'LL NEED: Copies of invitation and utensil tags (page 140), deputy and sheriff badges (page 141), and WANTED poster (page 142) on colored cardstock paper for each daddy/daughter team.
SUPPLIES: Rope, straight or safety pins, camera, decoration and game supplies, pint jars, scissors, markers, and grub.
INVITATIONS: Make and deliver a week ahead.
DECORATIONS: Jail and Photo Booth. Option #1: Cover a large cardboard box with brown butcher paper and hang black crepe paper bars. Carve an opening door. Cut out and paint a cardboard silver key and keyhole. Write JAIL at the top. Option #2: Hang black crepe paper from a board arched between two bi-fold room dividers found at the church (6 feet apart). Place cardboard wall in front with swinging door (tape wall to a table or bench). Table Decorations. Cover tables with brown or sunflower yellow butcher paper, beans, straw, cowboy hats, an old boot, hats, rocks, twigs, and sunflowers in quart jars. To make placemats cut 11" x 14" placemats out of colored butcher paper or cardboard (painted brown). Make a denim pocket to enclose utensils, napkins, and Cowgirl and Cowboy Grub sign (or tie sign to utensils). Wanted Posters. Ahead of time, take photos of girls wearing cowgirl hats. Glue photo on WANTED poster (page 142). Frame poster by mounting it to brown butcher paper, and antique with brown paint smudges. Tie on jute bows and hanger, and hang on jail to decorate.
SHERIFF DAD & DEPUTY DAUGHTER DUTIES: Tell guests that any sheriff or deputy can make an arrest and put someone in jail for 30 seconds if these laws are not obeyed. Law #1 Say, "Sheriff" or "Deputy" before speaking that person's name. Give badges to guests as they arrive, placing last names on sheriff badges and first names on deputy badges. Law #2 Pardners must yell Ya-hoo! after each game.
ACTIVITIES: Dads and daughters line up to compete. Mark each race with two sets of markers 30 feet apart. Race to the mark and back to the finish line. Tell guests to yell "Yahoo!" at the end or go to jail! Give 12" licorice ropes, cow toffee or taffy, or Western Sugar Cookies* to participants.
#1 Wheelbarrow Race. Dads race by placing daughter in wheelbarrow, or dad holds daughter's legs and she walks on hands.
#2 3-Legged Race. Standing side-by-side, dad and daughter put one leg into gunnysack, or tie inside legs together. Mark beginning and finish line, say go! "Yahoo!"
#3 Potato Jog. Each daddy and daughter team race the other team by placing a potato between their legs and racing to the marker and back to finish line. If potato drops, start from where you dropped potato and go! "Yahoo!"
#4 Cattle Rustlin' Tug of War. Have the bishop or leader pose as the U.S. Marshal to give these orders: *"Line up, dudes! It's time to gather up some cattle rustlers. We at _____ County are tired of losin' our cattle. We must find out who has been doin' these disasterly deeds! Let's have a rope pullin' contest. Team up with your sheriff and deputy partner. Divide into two teams and pull! The losers are the true cattle thieves and they must go to jail!"* "Yahoo!"
Other Fun Activities: Horseshoe pitching, Cinderella Cowgirl play (page 50), square dancing, western swing or line-dancing, watermelon or pie eating contest. Take photos of dad and daughter in front of jailhouse. To frame photos, make a copy of framed invitation (page 140), cutting out all words accept "Dad and Me Western Jamboree."
COWBOY & COWGIRL GRUB IDEAS: Pie Tin Supper Ideas. Sloppy Joes, pork and beans, olives, potato chips, ice cream, potato salad, corn-on-the-cob, fried chicken legs and rootbeer (served in pint jars). Dessert Ideas. Brownies, Strawberry Shortcake, Rootbeer Floats, or *Western Styled Sugar Cookies (star and horseshoe shapes, frosted, adding chocolate chip horseshoe nails). Favor: Trailmix

WANTED!
Sheriff Dad &
Deputy Daughter
to report for duty
at the
WESTERN
JAMBOREE!

Date: _____ Time: _____
Place: _____

Don't forget to wear your western garb!

Cowboy & Cowgirl
GRUB STICKS
Dig in with this
pitchfork, shovel
and plow... and
lick your lips
WRANGLER style!
Yippi-i-o-Ki-ay!

PATTERN: Sheriff Dad and Deputy Daughter badges . . . . Dad and Me Western Jamboree

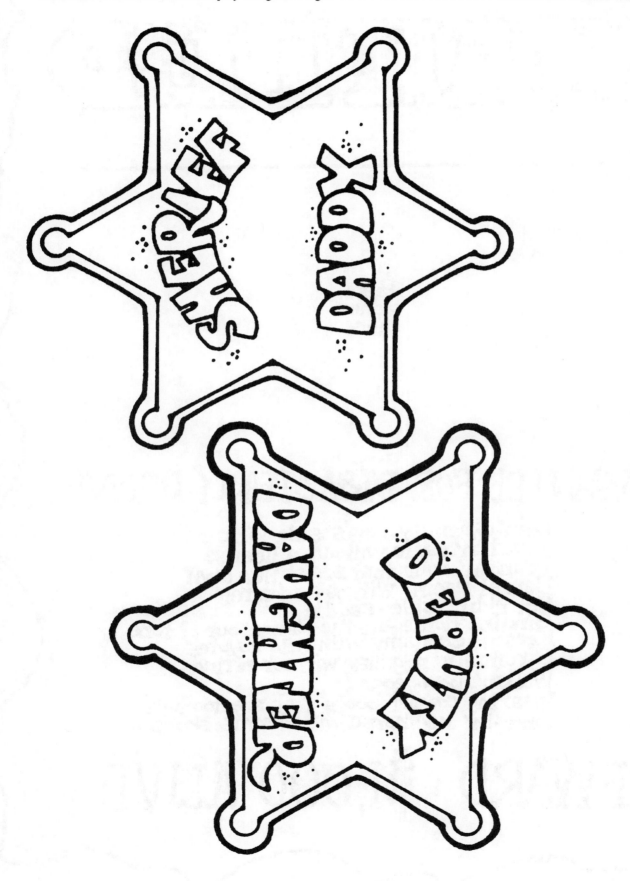

"WANTED"

_____

Paste
picture
here

WANTED FOR DISASTERLY DEEDS!

Bein' Calamity Jane's side-kick
Rustlin' cattle without a license
Brandin' bulls that aren't her own
Barrel racin' without a barrel
Not ridin' side-saddle
Singin' "Home-on-the-Range" out of tune
Keepin' company with wild coyotes
Strummin' a guitar without strings
Walkin' bow-legged
Wearing cowgirl boots that are too tight
Shoe-in' her horse with tennis shoes

REWARD : $1,000 ALIVE !

Party #4 THEME: *Mom and Miss "Pig"nic: Mother and Daughter Social*

YOU'LL NEED: 1. Copies of invitation (page 144).
2. Copies of Mom and Miss "Pig"nic! photo frame and Pig-nic Manners favor (page 145) on colored cardstock paper for each mother and daughter team.
3. Copies of Let's Pig Out! pig trough label (page 146).
4. Photos of mother and one of daughter to enclose in frame.
5. PLUS: Pink curling ribbon, 1 paper plate and 4 wooden craft sticks (for trough) for each guest, 1 Big Hunk or Butterfinger candy bar for each mother and daughter team (to place in trough), extra candy bars or snack treats for winners on the Oink Opinions game, and "Pig"nic treats (below).

INVITATION: Color, cut out and deliver two weeks ahead. Punch hole on card by tail and tie on pink curly ribbon. Invitation asks girls to bring blanket.

BEFORE: 1) Decorate a table to place "Pig"nic food on. Ideas: Curl pink ribbon to make 3" pink pig tails and tape to and spread out on top of table. Enlarge pig illustrations, color and cut out and glue to front of table. Decorate sides of table by tying pink and green helium-filled balloons with pink curly ribbon to the table. Decorate room with a few picnic baskets. 2) Make Let's Pig-Out! troughs for each mother/daughter team. 3) Collect or take photos of mother and daughter ahead of time. Color Memories of Mom and Miss "Pig"nic! frame, cut out pig faces and tape photo behind frame (faces peering through).

DURING: 1) Have girls place blanket on floor. 2) Give each mother and daughter team a Let's Pig Out! pig trough and Pig-nic Manners favor. 3) Sing *Swinging on a Star* and The Ants Go Marching.* 4) Play Oink Opinions detailed below. 5) Pig-out serving the "Pig"nic items below. Option: To save money each mother/daughter team could bring their own picnic. 6) Give each mother/daughter team their photo. 7) Other Fun Options: Play the game Pass the Pig or watch the Oscar-winning pig movie, BABE!

TO MAKE LET'S PIG-OUT! TROUGH: Fold a paper plate in half and staple bottom left and right edges together, leaving the top open. Glue a wooden craft stick on front and back on each end crossing sticks. Cut out and glue the Let's Pig Out! label (page 144) on front. Make one for mother and one for daughter. Place a candy bar in each and fill with popcorn. Candy Bar Ideas: Big Hunk (write and cut out a the letter "P" and place over the "B" to read "Pig Hunk," or a Butterfinger bar (write and cut out the word "Muddy" and place over Butter to read "Muddy" Finger. Use your imagination.

OINK OPINIONS: Play the dating-like or newly-wed-like game where 4 mothers go out and 4 daughters sit in chairs. Ask 4 questions to girls to see how well they know their mothers. Then bring in mothers and ask the same questions to see if mothers answer the question the same as their daughter. Then switch places. Award candy bars or snack treat to winning mother/daughter team. Question Ideas: Favorite color, treat, movie, color of toothbrush, shoes, memorable moment with you, best girlfriend, hobby, talent, food, pet, store, cartoon, joke, pizza topping, ice cream topping, restaurant. Most embarrassing moment. Best date with dad. Christmas tradition. The type of gift she usually asks for.

"PIG"NIC: <u>Pigs in a Blanket</u>. Cut ready-made bread stick dough strips in half and wrap around a hot dog cut in half with pig's head poking out 1". Bake 350° for 20-25 minutes or until golden brown. Serve with catsup, mustard, or other condiments. Serve with potato chips, olives, and carrots. <u>Pig Face Cupcakes</u>. Frost cupcakes with peach (light orange/red) frosting. MAKE A FACE: NOSE--Smash a giant red gumdrop flat (1 1/2") with a rolling pin. Pierce two snout holes with a straw and place at bottom of cupcake. EYES--Cut tops off two small green gumdrops and place above snout. EARS--Smash two small red gumdrops ear shape 1/2" and place in frosting at top. <u>Ants on a Log</u>. Cut celery into 5" pieces, fill with peanut butter, and top with raisins.

*Swinging on a Star by Johnny Burke, Music by Jimmy Van Heusen, Copyright 1944 by Bourne Co. & Dorsey Bros. Music.

"PIG"NIC MANNERS

Dance a pig-jig when the ants come.
Sing at the trough and suck your thumb (hoof).
Roll in mud and squeel and drool,
so everyone will think you're real cool!
Say "sweeee-t" instead of "please,"
and open your snout and sneeze!
Hog down with hoofs on the table,
then forget to thank Aunt Mabel.

by Ima Hog and S.N. Ort

Let's Pig-out!

Pigs porridge hot....
Pigs porridge cold....
Pigs porridge in the trough.
Nine days old.

Party #5 THEME: Burstin' with Pride! - Achievement Recognition

OBJECTIVE: Invite parents and family to share the excitement of Achievement Day goals achieved. Activity allows girls to wear bandelo, show notebooks, and tell about goals achieved.

YOU'LL NEED: Copies of award certificate (page 148) on colored cardstock for each girl, balloons for games and table decorations, and Success Snacks.

INVITATIONS: Have girls blow up a balloon and write the invitation on the balloon, then deflate balloon and give balloon invitation to their family to blow up and read. Invitation balloon reads: Come to a Balloon Bustin' AD Awards Party!, Date, Time, Place.

DECORATIONS: Have girls decorate several balloons to match the Achievement Days balloons on the bandelo. Place decorated balloons on tables or mount on the wall with heavy tape. To make arms on the balloons twist long, skinny balloons around the base. Decorate refreshment table with 12 helium-filled balloons and number them 1-12 to represent the 12 goal areas.

AWARD ACTIVITIES: Allow girls to show-and-tell about their goals and awards.
1. <u>Journal Display</u>: Have girls show parents their Achievement Days journal and tell what they did during the year. This could be done at their balloon-decorated table.

2. <u>Goal Guess and Tell</u>: Girls take parents from table to table to look at the decorated balloons, to guess which goal area the balloons represent, i.e. Arts and Crafts balloon would be holding a pair of scissors, and the Personal Preparedness balloon would be holding a watch.
3. <u>Award Burstin' with Pride! Certificates</u>: Using a calligraphy pen, fill out the certificate ahead and present to each girl in front of their family.
4. <u>Awards Bandelo and/or Poster</u>: Girls can wear their bandelo (pages 4-5, 24) to the activity and while they are receiving their awards certificate. They can show the jewels, sequins, pearls, or stickers earned on their awards poster.

POP INTO THE

FUTURE! ACTIVITY: Follow the activity instructions from Party #1 (page 1) to review the My Achievement Days* book, and then allow parents or older family members to take the Pop-Quiz (page 6). Divide into teams with daughter observing. Parents compete, popping balloons, reading the goal clues found inside the balloons, and then guessing the goal area. If girls did not have a chance to do this activity in Party #1, they may want to join their parents in the competition.

SUCCESS SNACKS: <u>Balloon Gumdrop Cupcakes</u>. Make cupcakes and frost with confetti frosting (add multi-colored decorator candy pieces to frosting), and top with gumdrop balloons. Smash small gumdrops into 1" round/flat shapes. Place gumdrop balloon at top of cupcake. Decorate balloon knot and string with dark colored frosting (place in plastic bag, cut a hole in one end and squeeze frosting through).

*My Achievement Days is published by The Church of Jesus Christ of Latter-day Saints, Salt Lake City, Utah.

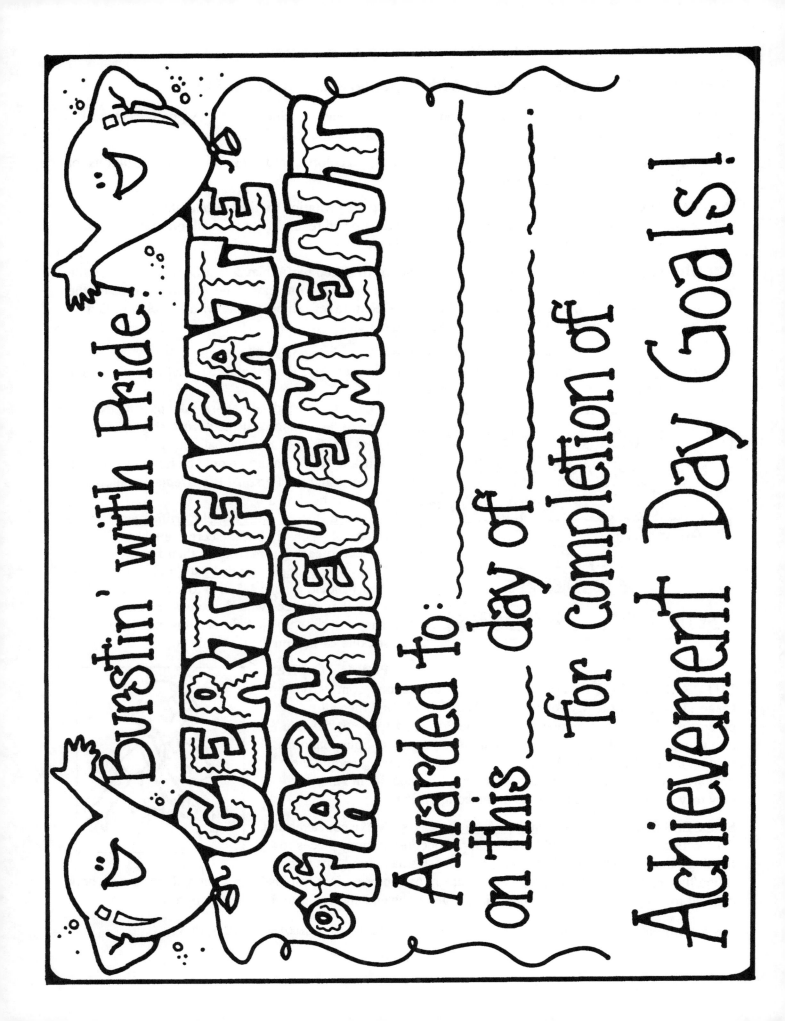

Mary H. Ross, Author and
Jennette Guymon-King, Illustrator
are the creators of

Primary Partners Books & CD-ROMS:
Lesson Match Activities and More:
Nursery and Age 3 (Sunbeams) Vol. 1 + CD-ROM
Nursery and Age 3 (Sunbeams) Vol. 2 + CD-ROM
CTR A and CTR B Ages 4-7 + CD-ROM
Book of Mormon Ages 8-11 + CD-ROM
Old Testament Ages 8-11 + CD-ROM
New Testament Ages 8-11 + CD-ROM
Doctrine & Covenants Ages 8-11 + CD-ROM
Achievement Days, Girls Ages 8-11 + CD-ROM
Quick-and-Easy Achievement Days + CD-ROM
Primary Partners Clip-Art on CD-ROM
Sharing Time, Singing Fun, Teaching Tools (for current year) + CD-ROM

Family Home Evening Books and CD-ROMS:
File Folder Family Home Evenings + CD-ROM
Home-spun Fun Family Home Evenings Vol 1 & 2 + CD-ROMs
Gospel Fun Activities, Gospel Fun Games + CD-ROM

Young Women Books and CD-ROMS:
Young Women Fun-tastic! Activities for Manuals 1, 2, and 3 + CD-ROMs
Young Women Fun-tastic! Personal Progress Motivators + CD-ROM

Mary Ross, Author
Mary Ross is an energetic mother, and has been a Primary teacher, and Achievement Days leader. She loves to help children and young women have a good time while learning. She has studied acting, modeling, and voice. Her varied interests include writing, creating activities and children's parties, and cooking. Mary and her husband, Paul, live with their daughter, Jennifer, in Sandy, Utah.

Jennette Guymon-King, Illustrator
Jennette Guymon-King studied graphic arts and illustration at Utah Valley State College and the University of Utah. She served a mission in Japan. Jennette enjoys sports, reading, cooking, art, gardening, and freelance illustrating. Jennette and her husband Clayton, live in Riverton, Utah. They are the proud parents of their daughter Kayla Mae, and sons Levi and Carson.

More *Primary Partners* Books for Ages 8-11
The following books also coordinate with lessons in Primary manuals*.

Book of Mormon
Primary 4 Manual*

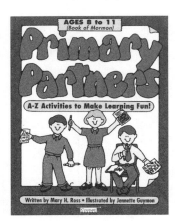

Doctrine & Covenants
Primary 5 Manual*

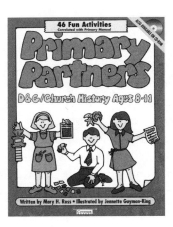

Old Testament
Primary 6 Manual*

You'll Find These and More:

- Book of Mormon Challenge Chart
- Wilderness Journey Object Find
- 3-D Tree of Life Box
- Nephi Ship Shape family Goal Chart
- My Personal Title of Liberty
- Waters of Mormon
- Alma the Younger's Repentance Maze
- Who is Abinadi? Poster
- King Lamoni's Father Scripture Story Match
- Book of Mormon Honor Roll Merit Match
- Cycle of History Wheel
- Moroni and Me Personal Golden Plates
- Weapons of War Buried for Peace Pop-up Quiz
- Sign Seekers Show-and-Tell
- CTR Commitment Calendar

You'll Find These and More:

- Apostasy Mirror Puzzle
- Then and Now Match Game
- "Note"able Hymns
- Revelation Routes
- Bishop Bingo
- Gifts of the Spirit Cross Match
- Standard Works Think-athon
- Premortal/earth Life Quiz
- Missionary Stretch Chart
- Choices & Consequences Cross Match
- Tracing My Ancestors Pedigree Chart
- Zion or Bust! Handcart Checklist
- Pioneer Word Find
- Sabbath Day Decision
- TESTIMONY Word Race
- Temple Light Poster
- Ordinance Opportunity Game

You'll Find These and More:

- Plan of Salvation Story Board Quiz
- Days 1-7 Creation Scripture Puzzle
- Noah and the Ark Word Search
- My Circle of Love Spin-and-Serve Game
- Eternal Choices Thumb Puppets
- Honesty Pays Blessings Bucks Board Game
- Egyptian Plagues Crossword
- 10 Commandments Key Word Cake
- My Personal Goliaths Prayer Journal
- Millennium Match Game
- Blessings Blockbuster
- Follow Righteous Leaders Trust-and-Tell
- Portrait of Spiritual Hero
- Humble Harry Humility Search